ASS A 2 / 2

225 lb/sq in.
50 sq ft.
101 ton 10 cwt. (with Diagram 106A boiler)
60 tons 7 cwt.
36' 11"
16' 0"
72' 8⅜"
6' 2"
Three 20" x 26"
Walschaerts with 10" piston valves

GRESLEY CLASS A^

Boiler pressure	2
Grate area	4
Weight: Engine	9
Tender	
Engine wheelbase	
Tender wheelbase	16' 0
Total length over buffers	See Gresley A1
Driving wheels	6' 8"
Cylinders	Three 19" x 26"
Motion	Walschaerts/Gresley with 8" piston valves

ASS A2/1

225 lb/sq in.
41.25 sq ft.
98 tons
52 tons
60 tons 7 cwt.
36' 8"
13' 6"
16' 0"
69' 5⅛" with 6-wheeled tender
71' 5⅛" with 8-wheeled tender
6' 2"
Three 19" x 26"
Walschaerts with 10" piston valves

THOMPSON CLASS A1/1

Boiler pressure	250 lb/sq in
Grate area	41.25 sq ft.
Weight: Engine	101 tons 10 cwt.
Tender	57 tons 18 cwt.
Engine wheelbase	38' 5"
Tender wheelbase	16' 0"
Total length over buffers	73' 2⅛"
Driving wheels	6' 8"
Cylinders	Three 19" x 26"
Motion	Walschaerts with 10" piston valves

LASS A1

250 lb/sq in.
50 sq ft.
104 tons 2 cwt.
105 tons 4 cwt. with roller bearings
60 tons 7 cwt.
60 tons 18 cwt. with roller bearings
36' 3"
16' 0"
72' 11¾"
6' 8"
Three 19" x 26"
Walschaerts with 10" piston valves

PEPPERCORN CLASS A2

Boiler pressure	250 lb/sq in.
Grate area	50 sq ft.
Weight: Engine	101 tons
Tender	60 tons 7 cwt.
Engine wheelbase	34' 4"
Tender wheelbase	16' 0"
Total length over buffers	71' 0¾"
Driving wheels	6' 2"
Cylinders	Three 19" x 26"
Motion	Walschaerts with 10" piston valves

POWER OF THE
A1s, A2s and A3s

Plate 1: Above   Gresley Class A3 No. 60086 *Gainsborough* with double chimney. It is seen having its tender replenished at Holbeck MPD, Leeds on 14th March 1961.

G. W. Morrison

Plate 2: Above   A scene inside the roundhouse at York on 6th February 1965 with Peppercorn Class A1 No. 60152 *Holyrood* awaiting its next duty.

G. W. Morrison

POWER OF THE
A1s, A2s
and A3s

J.S. Whiteley and G.W. Morrison

Oxford Railway Publishing Co.

ISBN 0 86093 133 1

Plate 3: Above   Peppercorn Class A1 No. 60154 *Bon Accord.*

G. W. Morrison

Plate 4: Below   Gresley Class A3 No. 60038 *Firdaussi.*

G. W. Morrison

Printed in Great Britain by
Blackwells Ltd, Oxford

Published by:
Oxford Publishing Co.
Link House
West Street
POOLE, Dorset

INTRODUCTION

The first tender locomotive of 4-6-2 wheel arrangement designed for use on the East Coast main line was *Great Northern*, Gresley's pioneer Pacific which was built for the GNR in 1922, just before the formation of the LNER. Raven was quick to follow with a Pacific design for the NER, and this wheel arrangement was perpetuated by successive Chief Mechanical Engineers of the LNER for locomotives required to handle the principal main line services.

This book has been prepared to show the development of these non-streamlined Pacific designs from the period immediately before the grouping, throughout the 25 years' existence of the LNER, and finally in the years after nationalisation of Britain's railways.

We are indebted to the photographers who have so kindly allowed us to use their pictures, and we would also like to thank Janet Blackburn for typing the manuscript.

CONTENTS

GRESLEY CLASS A1

Original No.	1924 or later No.	First 1946 No.	Second 1946 No.	BR No.	Built	Name	Subsequent Name	Maker	Works No.	Class A10	Rebuilt to A3
1470	4470 3/25				4/1922	Great Northern		Doncaster	1536		*
1471	4471 7/25				7/1922	Sir Frederick Banbury		Doncaster	1539		10/42
1472	4472 2/24	502 1/46	103 5/46		2/1923	Flying Scotsman		Doncaster	1564	5/45	1/47
1473	4473 6/24				3/1923	Solario		Doncaster	1565		10/41
1474	4474 11/24				3/1923	Victor Wild		Doncaster	1566		10/42
1475	4475 2/25		106 5/46		4/1923	Flying Fox		Doncaster	1567	5/45	3/47
1476	4476 2/25				5/1923	Royal Lancer		Doncaster	1568	5/45	10/46
1477	4477 6/25				6/1923	Gay Crusader		Doncaster	1569		1/43
1478	4478 2/25				7/1923	Hermit		Doncaster	1570		11/43
1479	4479 3/25				7/1923	Robert the Devil		Doncaster	1571		8/42
1480N	4480 4/25				8/1923	Enterprise		Doncaster	1572		7/27
1481N	4481 7/25	511 1/46	112 5/46		9/1923	St. Simon		Doncaster	1573	5/45	8/46
2543			44 9/46		6/1924	Melton		Doncaster	1598	5/45	9/47
2544					7/1924	Lemberg		Doncaster	1600		12/27
2545					8/1924	Diamond Jubilee		Doncaster	1601		8/41
2546			47 9/46		8/1924	Donovan		Doncaster	1602	5/45	1/48
2547					8/1924	Doncaster		Doncaster	1603	5/45	5/46
2548					9/1924	Galtee More		Doncaster	1604	5/45	10/45
2549					10/1924	Persimmon		Doncaster	1605		12/43
2550					10/1924	Blink Bonny		Doncaster	1606	5/45	11/45
2551					11/1924	Prince Palatine		Doncaster	1607		8/41
2552					11/1924	Sansovino		Doncaster	1608		9/43
2553					12/1924	Manna	Prince of Wales 11/26	Doncaster	1609		7/43
2554					12/1924	Woolwinder		Doncaster	1610		6/42
2555					2/1925	Centenary		Doncaster	1611		8/44
2556			57 9/46		2/1925	Ormonde		Doncaster	1612	5/45	1/47
2557					2/1925	Blair Athol		Doncaster	1613	5/45	12/45
2558					3/1925	Tracery		Doncaster	1614		7/42
2559					4/1925	The Tetrarch		Doncaster	1615		1/42
2560					4/1925	Pretty Polly		Doncaster	1616		5/44
2561					5/1925	Minoru		Doncaster	1617		6/44
2562					7/1925	Isinglass		Doncaster	1618	5/45	4/46
2563					8/1924	William Whitelaw	Tagalie 7/41	N.B. Loco	23101		11/42
2564			65 10/46		8/1924	Knight of the Thistle	Knight of Thistle 12/32	N.B. Loco	23102	5/45	3/47
2565					8/1924	Merry Hampton		N.B. Loco	23103	5/45	12/45
2566					8/1924	Ladas		N.B. Loco	23104		11/39
2567			68 8/46	60068 9/48	9/1924	Sir Visto		N.B. Loco	23105	5/45	12/48
2568					9/1924	Sceptre		N.B. Loco	23106		5/42
2569		538 3/46	70 6/46		9/1924	Gladiateur		N.B. Loco	23107	5/45	1/47
2570					9/1924	Tranquil		N.B. Loco	23108		10/44
2571					9/1924	Sunstar		N.B. Loco	23109		7/41
2572					10/1924	St. Gatien		N.B. Loco	23110	5/45	11/45
2573					10/1924	Harvester		N.B. Loco	23111		4/28
2574					10/1924	St. Frusquin		N.B. Loco	23112		6/42
2575					10/1924	Galopin		N.B. Loco	23113		6/41
2576					10/1924	The White Knight		N.B. Loco	23114		7/43
2577					10/1924	Night Hawk		N.B. Loco	23115		1/44
2578					10/1924	Bayardo		N.B. Loco	23116		5/28
2579					11/1924	Dick Turpin		N.B. Loco	23117		11/42
2580					11/1924	Shotover		N.B. Loco	23118		2/28
2581					11/1924	Neil Gow		N.B. Loco	23119		1/43
2582					12/1924	Sir Hugo		N.B. Loco	23120		12/41

* No. 4470 was rebuilt to Thompson A1 class in September 1945 (see Section 6)

Towards the end of 1911 Herbert Nigel Gresley (Sir Nigel Gresley from 1936) was appointed Locomotive Engineer of the Great Northern Railway. He held this post until 1923 when he was made Chief Mechanical Engineer of the newly formed LNER, a position he then held for eighteen years until he died in office on 5th April 1941.

As soon as he took up office at Doncaster on the GNR, succeeding H. A. Ivatt who had developed his famous Atlantic designs, Gresley showed interest in designing a larger and more powerful express passenger locomotive than Ivatt's large boilered Atlantics, thus perpetuating the GNR 'big engine' tradition. In 1913 drawings were prepared for a four-cylinder simple Atlantic and in 1915 one of the large boilered Atlantics, No. 279, was rebuilt as a four-cylinder simple engine with Walschaerts valve gear, a design which he was able to evaluate in connection with his thoughts for a new Pacific. Two different proposals were then considered for Pacific designs, the first essentially an enlarged version of No. 279, and the second having a slightly lighter axle loading and a boiler with a narrower firebox.

In the event, however, neither Pacific design was pursued as Gresley's thoughts turned to three-cylinder designs with con-jugated valve gear to operate the valve on the middle cylinder.

His first three-cylinder engine appeared in May 1918, Class O2 2-8-0 No. 461. Following its success, further three-cylinder designs were considered and in 1920 his large boilered three-cylinder 2-6-0 express goods engine appeared with a simpler form of conjugated valve gear.

Gresley then concentrated on his design for an express passenger engine, and on 19th January 1921 Doncaster Works received authority to build two Pacifics for the GNR with Gresley's proud claim that he had designed them to haul passenger train loads of up to 600 tons on the East Coast main line. The first of his three-cylinder Class A1 Pacifics, No. 1470, aptly named Great Northern, was completed on 30th March 1922 and entered traffic on 11th April. The second engine, No. 1471, entered traffic three months later on 10th July, the very same day that a further ten were ordered, all of which were completed by the LNER in 1923. After Gresley had taken up office as Chief Mechanical Engineer of the LNER forty more of his taper boiler Pacifics of 180lb/sq in working pressure were ordered, making a total of fifty-two engines built between April 1922 and July 1925. Section Three deals with subsequent alterations and improvements to his A1 Pacifics.

Plate 5: Above   The frames were laid for Gresley's pioneer Pacific on 26th August 1921 and it was completed on 30th March 1922. It entered traffic on 11th April 1922 named *Great Northern* and was only the second GNR engine ever to be named. Gresley had designed his new class of Pacific to haul passenger train loads as heavy as 600 tons and the appearance of *Great Northern* heralded the advent of a new era of locomotive design and performance on the East Coast main line. The new Pacific is seen under construction at Doncaster on 24th January 1922 with the boiler and major fittings positioned on the main frame.

Courtesy National Railway Museum

Plate 6: Below   Great Northern was followed by No. 1471 which entered traffic on 10th July 1922, and on that same day an order was placed for a further ten A1 Pacifics which were numbered 1472–1479, 1480N and 1481N when they entered service during 1923. With the exception of No. 1481N, all twelve of these A1 Pacifics were built to the generous GNR loading gauge, but during construction No. 1481N was altered to conform to the North British loading gauge. Between February 1928 and September 1933 the other eleven were altered to the LNER composite loading gauge, to which the remainder of the class were built. No. 1471 was named *Sir Frederick Banbury* late in 1923 after the last Chairman of the GNR. Together with No. 1470 it was turned out in the standard GNR passenger green livery, as seen here, and all the other A1s were given LNER green livery when put into service. No. 1470 was changed to LNER livery in October 1923 and No. 1471 in December 1923.

Courtesy National Railway Museum

Plate 7: Above   A further forty A1s were ordered late in 1923, twenty of which were built at Doncaster and twenty at N.B. Loco Co. The first of the batch from N.B.Loco Co., No. 2563 is seen nearing completion on the crane inside Hyde Park Works in 1924, with No. 2568 on steam test. No. 2563 was at first named *William Whitelaw*, and out of a total of fifty-two A1s was one of only four named when first entering traffic (see also *Plate 26*).

NELPG Collection

Plate 8: Right   The first twelve A1s were all completed before the LNER group numbering scheme was implemented in February 1924, and as such were given the numbers 1470—1481 in the GNR series, although an N suffix was in fact added to the last two, Nos. 1480 and 1481. All twelve were given their LNER numbers 4470—4481 between February 1924 and July 1925. No. 1475 is seen at Grantham before it was re-numbered 4475 in February 1925 and before it was named *Flying Fox*. Note the original position of the number on the tender together with the lettering L & NER. The front footsteps which were initially fitted to Nos. 1472—1481N are also visible (see also *Plate 10*).

T. G. Hepburn

boiler pressure, in which the GWR locomotives fared rather better than the A1s and were more economical on coal consumption, Gresley looked into the possibilities of improving the short-travel valve gear on his A1s. No.4477 *Gay Crusader* was selected as the first A1 to have valve gear alterations, but only minimum alteration was made which was not thought to be entirely successful. After improvements were made, the new long-travel valve gear was fitted to No. 2555 *Centenary* which emerged from Doncaster Works on 25th March 1927. It immediately showed an appreciable saving in coal, and performed considerably better than the other Pacifics. Instructions were therefore issued on 14th May 1927 to have all the Pacifics fitted with this improved valve gear which resulted in the engines being fitted with extended casings around the outside steam pipes as can be seen in this picture of No. 4479 *Robert the Devil* taken at Grantham in 1930.

A. C. Cawston

Plate 9: Above Following the results of the famous locomotive exchange trials in April and May 1925 between Nos. 4474/5 and two GWR 'Castle' Class 4-6-0s with their long-travel valves and 225 lb/sq in

Plate 10: Right No. 4474 *Victor Wild* is seen at Grantham in 1931, still to GNR loading gauge but with the first alteration to the buffer beam following its accident at Newcastle Central station on 10th May 1927 when the front footsteps struck the edge of the platform. As the A1s commenced regular through running to Newcastle in July 1927, Gresley immediately had the front footsteps removed from Nos. 4473–80, those on Nos. 4481 and 4472 having been removed in 1924 and 1925 respectively.

A. C. Cawston

Plate 11: Left No. 4479 *Robert the Devil* is passing Potters Bar in 1936 on the 4.00pm Kings Cross–Leeds. By this date the bottom corners of the buffer beam have been cut away to a greater extent and it has been altered to the LNER loading gauge. The plate-backed front footsteps which were fitted to the A1s from 1935 can be seen in this picture, and the number has been transferred from the tender to the cab to allow interchangeability of the corridor tenders which were introduced in 1928 for non-stop running between Kings Cross and Edinburgh.

A. C. Cawston

Plate 12: Above   No. 1472 was the first of the second batch of A1s, and it had the distinction of being the first engine to be completed at Doncaster Works after the grouping. It entered traffic on 24th February 1923, was renumbered 4472 and named *Flying Scotsman* in February 1924 for its appearance at the British Empire Exhibition at Wembley, for which it was given the LNER official coat of arms which can be seen on the cabside. In this picture the short-travel valve gear can clearly be seen together with the large GNR chimney and high cab roof.

Courtesy National Railway Museum

Plate 13: Left   *Flying Scotsman* was given long-travel valve gear and was altered to LNER loading gauge in April 1928. It was attached to a corridor tender from April 1928 until October 1936 in connection with its use on non-stop services from Kings Cross to Edinburgh. It had the honour of heading the first non-stop 'Flying Scotsman' from Kings Cross to Edinburgh on 1st May 1928 and is seen here leaving Grantham on 10th May 1930 for an exhibition at Nottingham with Gresley's experimental Class W1 4-6-4, nicknamed the 'hush-hush', visible at the rear.

A. C. Cawston

Plate 14: Below   In Spring 1938 it is passing Ganwick heading an express for Scarborough attached to a GNR tender after its corridor tender had been transferred to one of the streamlined Class A4s which by this time were handling most of the non-stop workings. *Flying Scotsman* is the only survivor of Gresley's non-streamlined Pacifics and happily can still be seen on special workings.

C. R. L. Coles

WESTINGHOUSE ENGINES

Plate 15: Above Fifteen A1s, Nos. 2568–82, were ordered for work in the North Eastern Area and as a result were all dual fitted with Westinghouse brakes for engine tender and train, and vacuum ejector for train brake. The Westinghouse air compressors were mounted on the right-hand side of the boiler above the rear coupled wheel, as can be seen in this picture of No. 2582 *Sir Hugo* at Grantham after arrival on a morning express from Newcastle in 1930. The pyrometer lead from the smokebox can be seen, together with the North Eastern Area classification 4.6.2 on the buffer beam which took until the early 1930s to correct when Doncaster took over maintenance from Darlington.

A. C. Cawston

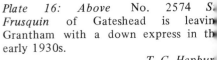

Plate 16: Above No. 2574 *St Frusquin* of Gateshead is leaving Grantham with a down express in the early 1930s.

T. G. Hepburn

Plate 17: Left Between 1933 and 1935 the Westinghouse equipment was removed from these fifteen engines following the Unification of Brake Programme which was started in 1924. No. 2571 *Sunstar* is seen at Grantham on an up express about 1930.

T. G. Hepburn

Plate 18: Above In August 1929 No. 2576 *The White Knight* was fitted with an A.C.F.I. feed water heater at Darlington Works following experiments with this apparatus with B12 4-6-0s and C7 Atlantics. Although it resulted in savings with coal and water, the cost of the apparatus and maintenance were questioned, and the apparatus was removed at Doncaster in December 1938. It is seen on shed at Grantham in 1930.

A. C. Cawston

AT WORK IN THE 1930s

Plate 19: Below In Spring 1938 No. 4475 *Flying Fox* is leaving Hadley Wood North Tunnel with an up Cup Final excursion.

C. R. L. Coles

Plate 20: Above   No. 2545 *Diamond Jubilee* is awaiting departure from Kings Cross in June 1938 and this was one of the twenty A1s built at Doncaster in 1924/5. It is attached to one of the ten streamlined non-corridor tenders which were built in 1936 and 1937 to replace the ten corridor tenders which were then being transferred to the streamlined A4s.

W. B. Greenfield, NELPG Collection

Plate 21: Below   Another of the 1924/5 Doncaster batch, No. 2547 *Doncaster*, is heading a heavy down Newcastle express near Hadley Wood in 1932. This was one of the three A1s in the Southern Area to be fitted with corridor tenders when they were first introduced in 1928, the other two being Nos. 4472 and 4476, and No. 2547 kept it until July 1933.

M. W. Earley

Plate 22: *Above*   A fine picture of No. 2548 *Galtee More* leaving Grantham with the 9.15 am to York on Grand National Day in 1932.

A. C. Cawston

Plate 23: *Below*   No. 2582 *Sir Hugo* was the last of the twenty A1s built by N.B. Loco Co., and it is seen near Potters Bar in 1938 heading an up Grantham express, having had its Westinghouse equipment removed in June 1933. The right-hand drive can clearly be seen in this picture, and although proposals for conversion to left-hand drive were considered in 1932, these were not implemented until after the engines were reboilered as Class A3.

C. R. L. Coles

Plate 24: Above   A scene inside Newcastle Central in 1938 showing No. 4476 *Royal Lancer* of Kings Cross attached to one of the new type non-corridor tenders, seventeen of which were initially built for new right-hand drive A3s from 1930, although some were subsequently transferred to A1s.

W. B. Greenfield, NELPG Collection

Plate 25: Below   An interesting picture taken at Newcastle Central on the wet evening of 9th December 1938 showing No. 2577 *Night Hawk* after arrival on the down 'Coronation', A4 Pacific No. 4483 *Kingfisher* having failed at Abbots Ripton.

W. B. Greenfield, NELPG Collection

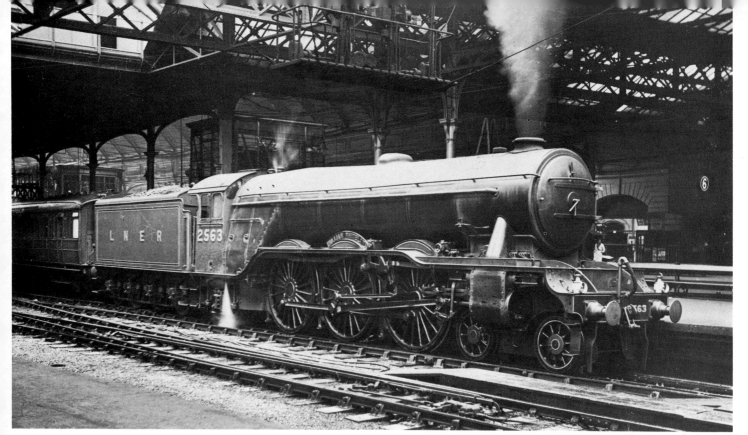

Plate 26: Above No. 2563 *William Whitelaw* standing on a down express at Newcastle Central on 16th July 1938. This engine was named after the Chairman of the LNER (renamed *Tagalie* in July 1941), and was one of only four A1s to be named when entering traffic, the others being the pioneer, *Great Northern*, No. 2555 *Centenary* which was the first engine completed at Doncaster in 1925, the Railway Centenary year, and No. 2562 *Isinglass*, the last A1 to be completed after the decision had been taken to name the whole class, mainly after racehorses.

W. B. Greenfield, NELPG Collection

Plate 27: Below Spectacular simultaneous departures from Newcastle Central on 2nd January 1939. Class A4 Pacific No. 4467 *Wild Swan* is starting the up 'Silver Jubilee' and No. 2581 *Neil Gow* a Liverpool express.

W. B. Greenfield, NELPG Collection

Plate 28: Above   This rear view, taken at Kings Cross in 1930, of two Pacifics about to separate and head their respective trains clearly shows the corridor tender attached to No. 2566 *Ladas*. These corridor tenders were designed to incorporate a passageway eighteen inches wide and five feet high on the right-hand side to allow a crew change in the middle of a non-stop journey between Kings Cross and Edinburgh, with the spare crew able to travel in comfort in the train for part of the journey. Ten were built for use with both A1s and A3s and were first attached to A1s Nos. 4472/6, 2547/56/69, and A3s Nos. 2573/80, 2743/4/5, the last three being the first three engines built as A3s. These tenders were interchangeable and were eventually fitted to a total of thirteen A1s and thirteen A3s before finally being transferred to the streamlined A4s from 1936. A3 No. 2750 *Papyrus* is in front of No. 2566 and was the last Gresley non-streamlined Pacific to be fitted with a corridor tender which it finally lost in September 1937.

A. C. Cawston

Plate 30: Above   On 19th July 1938 No. 4481 *St. Simon* is leaving York with the up 'Scarborough Flyer'. This engine was the last of the 1923 batch and during construction was altered from the proposed GNR loading gauge to the North British loading gauge. It did however retain the high ventilator on the cab roof, which can be seen in this picture, until January 1948 when it was transferred to A3 No. 66 *Merry Hampton* (see *Plate 66*).

J. P. Wilson

Plate 31: Right   An up express is approaching Potters Bar about 1930 behind No. 2546 *Donovan*.

N. Stead Collection

Plate 32: Right   Impressive motive power for a down express at Low Fell on 5th March 1939 with Worsdell Class C6 4-4-2 No. 697 piloting No. 4476 *Royal Lancer*.

W. B. Greenfield,
NELPG Collection

Plate 29: Opposite   No. 4475 *Flying Fox* is standing at Kings Cross in June 1938 whilst running in on a slow. The coupled driving wheels of these beautifully proportioned engines were six feet eight inches in diameter and how well these engines looked in their LNER apple green livery with black and white lining.

W. B. Greenfield,
NELPG Collection

Plate 33: Above   Following the introduction of Gresley's streamlined A4s, several A1s were transferred to Gorton, Leicester and Neasden for service over the Great Central Section. No. 4473 *Solario* is standing at Nottingham Victoria on 19th May 1939, having been transferred from Doncaster to Gorton earlier in the month. It is heading a Manchester—Marylebone express and at this period these trains were worked through without an engine change.

J. P. Wilson

Plate 34: Below   No. 4478 *Hermit* was another one of the A1s which was transferred to Gorton, in March 1939, and it is seen later in 1939 heading the 3.20pm Marylebone—Manchester express near Northwood on the former Metropolitan and GC joint line.

C. R. L. Coles

Plates 35 and *36*   Two more pictures of A1s on GC expresses, both taken by J. P. Wilson. In the upper picture No. 4473 *Solario* is accelerating away from Nottingham near New Basford on 19th June 1939 heading a down Manchester express, and below, No. 4478 *Hermit* is leaving Nottingham Victoria on 22nd June 1939 with a Manchester express.

As already described, the decision to fit the A1s with long travel valve gear was made in 1927, and the last engines to be dealt with were Nos. 2545 and 2557 in May 1931. The next major improvement to these engines was the fitting of new higher pressure boilers, also as a result of the exchange trials of 1925, and this is dealt with in Section Three.

RAVEN CLASS A2

No.	Name	Built	Maker	A1 Boiler Fitted	8-Wheel Tender	Withdrawn
2400	City of Newcastle	12/1922	Darlington	–	12/34	4/37
2401	City of Kingston upon Hull	12/1922	Darlington	–	10/34	7/36
2402	City of York	3/1924	Darlington	–	8/34	7/36
2403	City of Durham	3/1924	Darlington	–	11/34	5/37
2404	City of Ripon	3/1924	Darlington	9/29	1/35	2/37

The next Pacifics to be built by one of the LNER constituent Companies were to the design of Vincent Raven, and two were built for the North Eastern Railway shortly before the grouping. Although they were the largest engines built at Darlington for the NER they were certainly far from the best. Possibly the main reason for their rather disappointing performance was the fact that the design was rushed in an attempt to ensure that the NER had a Pacific before the Company lost its identity on the formation of the LNER on 1st January 1923.

The authority for these two Pacifics to be built was given to Darlington Works on 30th March 1922, the very same day that the first GNR Pacific, No. 1470, was completed at Doncaster, undoubtedly not a coincidence. No. 2400 was the first to be completed in December 1922, and No. 2401 followed later in the month but did not actually start running until January 1923. These three-cylinder engines were essentially an elongated version of Raven's very successful superheated Atlantics, the main differences being larger cylinders, larger diameter boiler, an extra pair of coupled wheels and a larger firebox. The drive from all three cylinders was to the leading coupled axle resulting in a long wheelbase of 37 feet 2 inches compared to the 35 feet 9 inches of the GNR Pacifics.

Three more engines were authorised very quickly, on 22nd February 1923. Whether this was because the results from the first two were thought to be satisfactory or because of Darlington's reaction to Gresley being appointed as Chief Mechanical Engineer of the newly formed LNER is questionable. However, Nos. 2402–4 appeared in March 1924, albeit with slight modifications authorised by Gresley. With Gresley appointed CME of the LNER, it is not surprising that his Pacifics were chosen for further construction following comparative tests in June and July 1923 between Raven Class A2 No. 2400 and Gresley Class A1 No. 1472. It has to be said, however, that the results of these tests were by no means conclusive, and some would suggest that No. 2400 produced rather better results than No. 1472. However, their fate was sealed and they were inevitably doomed to early withdrawal.

All five of these engines were allocated to Gateshead from new until being moved to York during 1934 where they stayed until withdrawal in 1936/7. Whilst at Gateshead they were almost entirely confined to the East Coast main line between Grantham and Edinburgh, making only very rare appearances at Kings Cross. After being transferred to York they were mainly used on heavy secondary passenger trains between there and Newcastle. None of the class achieved half a million miles and No. 2402 *City of York* had the dubious distinction of being the first locomotive built by the LNER to be scrapped, in July 1936, the last of the class being withdrawn from service in May 1937.

Plate 37: Below   The Raven A2s were designed to handle expresses between York and Edinburgh. They had three 19″ x 26″ cylinders, independent Stephenson valve gear, 6′ 8″ coupled wheels and a 200lb/sq in boiler. No. 2400 is seen at Darlington just after the grouping, still in lined North Eastern Passenger livery and unnamed.

Courtesy National Railway Museum

Plates 38 and *39*   Two pictures by A. C. Cawston of No. 2400 *City of Newcastle* arriving at Grantham and awaiting departure from the station with the up 'Flying Scotsman' in Spring 1930. At this period during the Winter Timetable the up 'Flying Scotsman' was a Gateshead lodging turn returning the following day with the down train. On this occasion No. 2400 was probably deputising for a failed Kings Cross A1, and as a result was making one of its rare appearances in London. No. 2400 received its LNER livery in July 1923, and all five A2s were named about March 1924. In these two pictures the Westinghouse brake pump can be seen together with the original six-wheeled NER standard tender which had a capacity of 5½ tons of coal and 4,125 gallons of water. Nos. 2400/1 had trailing wheels with inside bearings which were never altered, but the final three engines were built to incorporate outside frames and Cartazzi axleboxes on the trailing wheels under the firebox.

Plate 40: Left No. 2403 *City of Durham* is at York in the late 1920s, still with its original NER type buffers which were replaced by the LNER standard type on all five A2s between 1929 and 1933. It can also be seen with its number on the tender which was later moved to the cabside, and the NER classification 4.6.2. on the buffer beam. The A2s were always right-hand drive engines but the Westinghouse brakes were removed between November 1931 and April 1933.

T. G. Hepburn

Plate 41: Below A fine picture of No. 2401 *City of Kingston upon Hull* leaving Edinburgh Waverley in July 1932 with the up 'Queen of Scots' Pullman which at this time was a fairly regular turn for an A2 as far as Newcastle.

T. G. Hepburn

Plate 42: Bottom The one major alteration to the class was the reboiling of No. 2404 *City of Ripon* with a Gresley Diagram 94 A1 Class boiler of 180 lb/sq in which was spare at Darlington in 1929, and thus avoided a new boiler having to be made for a small class of engine which obviously had a limited life. No. 2404 emerged from Darlington Works in September 1929 with its A1 boiler which had been given a new firebox, and with a Doncaster-style cab. From the end of 1931, therefore No. 2404 became Class A2/2 and Nos. 2400/3 A2/1, the classifications which they retained until withdrawal. During 1934 all five were transferred to York to replace Atlantics on heavy secondary passenger trains between there and Newcastle, and No. 2404 is seen on one such duty leaving York about 1935. It is attached to a Gresley eight-wheeled new type non-corridor tender which were fitted to all five engines between August 1934 and January 1935. These tenders had an increased capacity of 8 tons of coal and 5,000 gallons of water and were transferred to Gresley A1s and A3s after the Raven A2s had been withdrawn. Their limited route availability, need for new boilers and the appearance of Gresley V2s led to early withdrawal, between July 1936 and May 1937.

T. G. Hepburn

GRESLEY CLASS A3

BR No.	Second 1946 No.	First 1946 No.	First No. as A3	Maker	Works No.	Built	Name	Rebuilt to A3	Double Chimney	Trough Deflectors	Withdrawn
60035 11/48	35 6/46	570 4/46	2500	Doncaster	1790	7/1934	Windsor Lad	Built as A3	1/59	—	9/61
60036 7/48	36 12/46		2501	Doncaster	1791	7/1934	Colombo	Built as A3	11/58	7/62	11/64
60037 10/48	37 8/46		2502	Doncaster	1792	7/1934	Hyperion	Built as A3	10/58	5/62	12/63
60038 6/48	38 10/46		2503	Doncaster	1793	8/1934	Firdaussi	Built as A3	9/59	—	11/63
60039 7/48	39 7/46		2504	Doncaster	1794	9/1934	Sandwich	Built as A3	7/59	6/61	3/63
60040 8/48	40 5/46	575 3/46	2505	Doncaster	1795	10/1934	Cameronian	Built as A3	10/59	3/62	7/64
60041 11/48	41 7/46		2506	Doncaster	1797	12/1934	Salmon Trout	Built as A3	7/59	1/63	12/65
60042 4/48	42 11/46		2507	Doncaster	1798	12/1934	Singapore	Built as A3	9/58	9/62	7/64
60043 8/48	43 8/46		2508	Doncaster	1800	2/1935	Brown Jack	Built as A3	2/59	2/62	5/64
60044 8/49	44 9/46		44	Doncaster	1598	6/1924	Melton	9/47	6/59	8/61	6/63
60045 6/48	45 11/46		2544	Doncaster	1600	7/1924	Lemberg	12/27	10/59	11/62	11/64
60046 8/49	46 7/46		2545	Doncaster	1601	8/1924	Diamond Jubilee	8/41	8/58	12/61	6/63
60047 5/48	47 9/46		47	Doncaster	1602	8/1924	Donovan	1/48	7/59	7/61	4/63
60048 11/48	48 5/46		48	Doncaster	1603	8/1924	Doncaster	5/46	5/59	12/61	9/63
60049 6/48	49 7/46	517 4/46	2548	Doncaster	1604	9/1924	Galtee More	10/45	3/59	10/60	12/62
60050 8/48	50 7/46	518 3/46	2549	Doncaster	1605	10/1924	Persimmon	12/43	4/59	10/61	6/63
60051 9/48	51 8/46		2550	Doncaster	1606	10/1924	Blink Bonny	11/45	8/59	3/62	11/64
60052 10/48	52 5/46	520 4/46	2551	Doncaster	1607	11/1924	Prince Palatine	8/41	11/58	10/62	1/66
60053 2/49	53 11/46	521 3/46	2552	Doncaster	1608	11/1924	Sansovino	9/43	11/58	—	5/63
60054 4/48	54 9/46	522 3/46	2553	Doncaster	1609	12/1924	Prince of Wales	7/43	8/58	5/62	6/64
60055 6/48	55 9/46		2554	Doncaster	1610	12/1924	Woolwinder	6/42	6/58	—	9/61
60056 5/49	56 7/46		2555	Doncaster	1611	2/1925	Centenary	8/44	7/59	8/61	5/63
60057 6/48	57 9/46		57	Doncaster	1612	2/1925	Ormonde	1/47	9/58	9/61	10/63
60058 3/49	58 12/46		2557	Doncaster	1613	2/1925	Blair Athol	12/45	10/58	—	6/63
60059 7/48	59 10/46		2558	Doncaster	1614	3/1925	Tracery	7/42	7/58	9/61	12/62
60060 10/48	60 6/46	528 4/46	2559	Doncaster	1615	4/1925	The Tetrarch	1/42	3/59	—	9/63
60061 11/48	61 11/46		2560	Doncaster	1616	4/1925	Pretty Polly	5/44	10/58	2/62	9/63
60062 7/49	62 10/46		2561	Doncaster	1617	5/1925	Minoru	6/44	2/59	7/61	12/64
60063 1/49	63 7/46	531 4/46	531	Doncaster	1618	7/1925	Isinglass	4/46	2/59	8/61	6/64
60064 7/49	64 10/46		2563	N.B. Loco	23101	8/1924	Tagalie	11/42	6/59	—	9/61
60065 7/48	65 10/46		65	N.B. Loco	23102	8/1924	Knight of Thistle	3/47	10/58	11/61	6/64
60066 3/48	66 7/46		2565	N.B. Loco	23103	8/1924	Merry Hampton	12/45	10/58	10/61	9/63
60067 7/48	67 10/46		2566	N.B. Loco	23104	8/1924	Ladas	11/39	4/59	7/61	12/62
60068 9/48			60068	N.B. Loco	23105	9/1924	Sir Visto	12/48	4/59	—	8/62
60069 7/48	69 5/46	537 3/46	2568	N.B. Loco	23106	9/1924	Sceptre	5/42	9/59	—	10/62
60070 8/48	70 6/46		70	N.B. Loco	23107	9/1924	Gladiateur	1/47	4/59	9/61	5/64
60071 5/48	71 10/46		2570	N.B. Loco	23108	9/1924	Tranquil	10/44	7/58	11/61	10/64
60072 8/48	72 7/46		2571	N.B. Loco	23109	9/1924	Sunstar	7/41	7/59	—	10/62
60073 3/49	73 10/46		2572	N.B. Loco	23110	10/1924	St. Gatien	11/45	8/58	7/61	8/63
60074 5/48	74 6/46	542 4/46	2573	N.B. Loco	23111	10/1924	Harvester	4/28	3/59	—	4/63
60075 5/48	75 10/46		2574	N.B. Loco	23112	10/1924	St. Frusquin	6/42	8/59	—	1/64
60076 9/48	76 9/46		2575	N.B. Loco	23113	10/1924	Galopin	6/41	6/59	—	10/62
60077 11/48	77 6/46	545 3/46	2576	N.B. Loco	23114	10/1924	The White Knight	7/43	4/59	7/61	7/64
60078 4/48	78 11/46		2577	N.B. Loco	23115	10/1924	Night Hawk	1/44	2/59	3/62	10/62
60079 3/48	79 11/46		2578	N.B. Loco	23116	10/1924	Bayardo	5/28	1/60	—	9/61
60080 3/49	80 11/46		2579	N.B. Loco	23117	11/1924	Dick Turpin	11/42	10/59	11/61	10/64
60081 6/48	81 12/46		2580	N.B. Loco	23118	11/1924	Shotover	2/28	10/58	—	10/62
60082 5/48	82 6/46		2581	N.B. Loco	23119	11/1924	Neil Gow	1/43	9/59	8/61	9/63
60083 5/49	83 10/46		2582	N.B. Loco	23120	12/1924	Sir Hugo	12/41	9/59	2/62	5/64
60084 5/48	84 10/46		2595	Doncaster	1731	2/1930	Trigo	Built as A3	7/58	1/62	11/64
60085 7/48	85 10/46		2596	Doncaster	1733	2/1930	Manna	Built as A3	11/58	4/62	10/64
60086 9/48	86 10/46		2597	Doncaster	1736	4/1930	Gainsborough	Built as A3	6/59	—	11/63
60087 10/48	87 10/46	565 3/46	2598	Doncaster	1743	6/1930	Blenheim	Built as A3	8/58	2/62	10/63
60088 7/48	88 8/46		2599	Doncaster	1744	7/1930	Book Law	Built as A3	7/59	6/61	10/63
60089 9/48	89 9/46		2743	Doncaster	1693	8/1928	Felstead	Built as A3	10/59	11/61	10/63
60090 2/49	90 12/46		2744	Doncaster	1694	8/1928	Grand Parade	Built as A3	8/58	1/63	Withdrawn
60091 4/48	91 10/46		2745	Doncaster	1695	9/1928	Captain Cuttle	Built as A3	3/59	10/61	10/64
60092 4/49	92 10/46		2746	Doncaster	1700	11/1928	Fairway	Built as A3	11/59	10/61	10/64
60093 9/48	93 7/46		2747	Doncaster	1703	12/1928	Coronach	Built as A3	12/58	—	4/62
60094 12/49	94 12/46		2748	Doncaster	1705	12/1928	Colorado	Built as A3	8/59	8/61	2/64
60095 9/48	95 5/46	558 3/46	2749	Doncaster	1707	2/1929	Flamingo	Built as A3	2/59	—	4/61
60096 10/48	96 11/46		2750	Doncaster	1708	3/1929	Papyrus	Built as A3	7/58	9/61	9/63
60097 6/48	97 5/46		2751	Doncaster	1709	4/1929	Humorist	Built as A3	7/37	—	8/63
60098 11/48	98 6/46	561 3/46	2752	Doncaster	1710	4/1929	Spion Kop	Built as A3	7/59	—	10/63
60099 7/49	99 7/46		2795	Doncaster	1738	4/1930	Call Boy	Built as A3	7/58	7/61	10/63
60100 4/49	100 7/46		2796	Doncaster	1741	5/1930	Spearmint	Built as A3	9/58	8/61	6/65
60101 8/48	101 7/46		2797	Doncaster	1742	6/1930	Cicero	Built as A3	2/59	—	4/63
60102 5/49	102 8/46		4471	Doncaster	1539	7/1922	Sir Frederick Banbury	10/42	4/59	—	11/61
60103 12/48	103 5/46		103	Doncaster	1564	2/1923	Flying Scotsman	1/47	1/59	12/61	1/63
60104 7/48	104 5/46		4473	Doncaster	1565	3/1923	Solario	10/41	4/59	—	12/59
60105 8/48	105 5/46		4474	Doncaster	1566	3/1923	Victor Wild	10/42	3/59	12/60	6/63
60106 12/48	106 5/46		106	Doncaster	1567	4/1923	Flying Fox	3/47	11/58	10/61	12/64
60107 4/48	107 10/46		107	Doncaster	1568	5/1923	Royal Lancer	10/46	6/59	2/62	9/63
60108 3/49	108 7/46	507 3/46	4477	Doncaster	1569	6/1923	Gay Crusader	1/43	5/59	11/61	10/63
60109 4/48	109 6/46	508 1/46	4478	Doncaster	1570	7/1923	Hermit	11/43	3/59	1/61	12/62
60110 3/49	110 8/46		4479	Doncaster	1571	7/1923	Robert the Devil	8/42	5/59	7/61	5/63
60111 10/49	111 5/46		4480	Doncaster	1572	8/1923	Enterprise	7/27	6/59	4/62	12/62
60112 3/49	112 5/46		112	Doncaster	1573	9/1923	St. Simon	8/46	7/58	10/62	12/64

Following the introduction of the Gresley Class A1 Pacifics, the East Coast passenger services were considerably improved, but at the expense of rather heavy coal consumption. As a result, alteration to longer travel valve gear was undertaken to the A1s, prompted by the superior performance of the GWR 'Castle' Class 4-6-0s, with their long-travel valves and higher boiler pressure of 225 lb/sq in, in the exchange trials of 1925, as described in Section One.

The cost of fitting this redesigned valve gear was minimal, but it proved extremely successful and reduced coal consumption to such an extent that all existing A1s had these alterations carried out as they passed through Works. The next major modification was made to these engines in 1927 when a decision was taken to increase the working pressure of their boilers from 180 lb/sq in to 220 lb/sq in incorporating large 43 element superheaters, again following the results of the 1925 exchange trials. On 11th March 1927 an order was placed at Doncaster for the first five of these boilers, the first one being fitted to No. 4480 *Enterprise* in July 1927, this engine then being reclassified A3. New 20″ diameter cylinders were also fitted to No. 4480 but these were subsequently reduced to 19″, although the second engine which was rebuilt to Class A3, No. 2544 *Lemberg*, was initially given 18¼″ cylinders with its high pressure boiler.

The success of these improvements convinced Gresley that all his existing A1 Pacifics should be rebuilt as Class A3 when new boilers were required, and all new construction of these engines should be to Class A3 with 220 lb/sq in boilers, 19″ diameter cylinders and long-travel valve gear. Construction of new A3s commenced with No. 2743 *Felstead* which entered service in August 1928. A total of twenty-seven A3s were built between 1928 and early 1935, all with left-hand drive unlike the earlier A1s which were all eventually altered from right-hand drive. Gradually all the A1 Pacifics (with the exception of No. 4470 *Great Northern* which is dealt with in Section Six) were rebuilt to Class A3, the last one being *Sir Visto* in December 1948 as BR renumbered 60068, which from May 1945 had been reclassified A10 together with sixteen other A1s to make way for Thompson's Pacifics.

During the remainder of their illustrious careers, the only other major changes to the A3s were the fitting of double chimneys to all seventy-eight engines, and smoke deflectors to fifty-five of the Class, this latter modification, whilst improving visibility from the footplate, was very much at the expense of the appearance of these beautifully proportioned engines.

Plate 43: Below   No. 2544 *Lemberg* was the second A1 to be reboilered as Class A3, in December 1927, and it is seen leaving Grantham in 1930 with a Newcastle–Kings Cross express. When No. 2544 was rebuilt with a higher pressure boiler its cylinders were specially lined to 18¼″ diameter, unlike any other A3, but in April 1932 it was fitted with new 19″ diameter cylinders to conform with the rest of the class.

A. C. Cawston

Plate 44: Above No. 2795 *Call Boy* was one of the twenty-seven engines built as Class A3 with 220 lb/sq in boiler, three 19″ x 26″ cylinders and left-hand drive. It was one of eight built in 1930, all of which were fitted with the newly designed New Type Non-Corridor tenders, but it is seen here in Summer 1932 near Saltersford on the up non-stop 'Flying Scotsman' paired with a corridor tender.

M. W. Earley

Plate 45: Below The final batch of nine A3s, Nos. 2500—8, were built between July 1934 and February 1935 and these were also fitted with New Type Non-Corridor tenders. No. 2504 *Sandwich* is passing Hornsey on a down express about 1939.

N. Stead Collection

Plate 46: Above   The last A3 to be built, No. 2508 *Brown Jack*, is passing Low Fell on 12th April 1939 with the up 'Queen of Scots' Pullman. The A3s could easily be distinguished from the earlier A1s by the protruding superheater header cover on the sides of the smokebox.

W. B. Greenfield, NELPG Collection

Plate 47: Below   A scene inside Newcastle Central about 1938 showing No. 2507 *Singapore* standing on the down 'Flying Scotsman'. This last batch of A3s were the first Pacifics to be given perforated steam collectors which could be distinguished by the 'banjo' dome on these Diagram 94A boilers.

W. B. Greenfield, NELPG Collection

NUMBER VARIATIONS

Plate 48: Right The Thompson renumbering scheme which was formulated in 1943 was put into practice in January 1946, but by April 1946 it was decided to renumber the A3s (and the remaining A1s which by then had been reclassified A10) in the sequence 35–112 in the same numerical order as their original LNER numbers. As a result only seventeen A3s ever received the interim 1946 number which had been allocated, one of them being No. 531 *Isinglass* seen here in wartime unlined black livery.

T. G. Hepburn

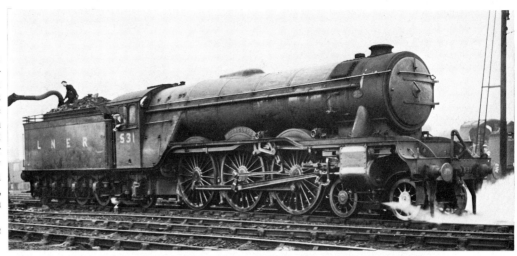

Plate 49: Above The 'banjo' dome can clearly be seen in this picture of *Fairway* at Grantham on 9th September 1948 with its second 1946 number, 92. The next change of numbers came after nationalisation when 60,000 was added to the second 1946 numbers between March 1948 and October 1949.

J. P. Wilson

Plate 50: Right In the first ten weeks after nationalisation on 1st January 1948, seven A3s were given a temporary E prefix to their numbers (Nos. 50, 62, 64, 72, 99, 103 and 112) before the addition of 60,000. No. E112 *St. Simon* is leaving Potters Bar Tunnel in May 1948 with the up 'Yorkshire Pullman'. It is still in LNER green livery but has 'British Railways' on the tender.

M. W. Earley

TRIALS AND SMOKE LIFTING EXPERIMENTS

Plate 51: Left No. 2751 *Humorist* was very much the guinea pig of the A3s and during its existence was the subject of many experiments. It is seen fitted with a test shield at Grantham in June 1931.

A. C. Cawston

Plate 52: Below Humorist leaving Grantham on a down trial run on 22nd June 1931.

A. C. Cawston

Plate 53: Bottom No. 2747 *Coronach* was the first A3 to be selected for alterations to its smokebox in connection with experiments to lift exhaust from the chimney clear of the cab and thus prevent the driver's view being obscured. In October 1931 it left Doncaster Works with the upper part of its smokebox partitioned off to form an air duct which discharged at the rear of the normal A3 chimney in two separate ducts in an attempt to effect an upward current of air, thus lifting the exhaust. After various trials it was not found to be entirely successful and in February 1933 the arrangements were removed from *Coronach* which is seen here on the turntable at Grantham in 1932. *A. C. Cawston*

Plate 54: Above A similar arrangement to that fitted to *Coronach* was fitted to *Humorist* in April 1932, but this time in conjunction with a new dual-chimney in which the air admitted at the top of the smokebox discharged through the rear half of the chimney. It is seen at Grantham in 1932, but as with No. 2747, the arrangement proved unsatisfactory and was removed later in 1932.

A. C. Cawston

Plate 55: Below Following trials in November 1932 with *Humorist* fitted with a semi-annular chimney, which was also unsatisfactory, the next scheme was tried with wind vanes fitted to the sides of the cut-away smokebox top and a stove-pipe chimney being fitted, as seen in this picture taken at Doncaster in March 1933. After further modification to the wind vanes it was felt that this smoke lifting experiment had proved reasonably successful, but strangely no further engines were dealt with, and *Humorist* reverted to normal in January 1934.

British Rail

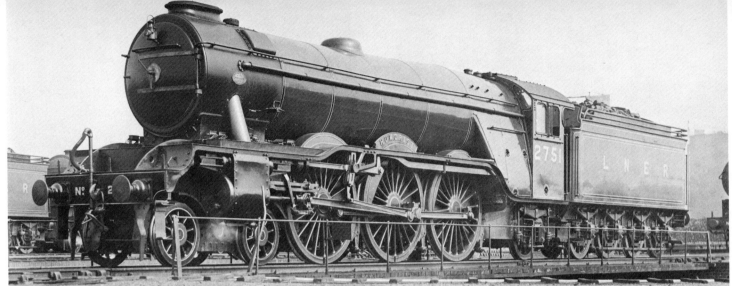

Plate 56: *Above* The next alteration to *Humorist* was in July 1937 when it was fitted with a double chimney and Kylchap blastpipe, following earlier trials with Class P2 2-8-2 No. 2001 *Cock o' the North* (see *Plate 143*). This was to be the most important modification to the A3s, and was later carried out with the entire class. The fitting of this double blastpipe arrangement resulted in *Humorist* being a particularly free-running and free-steaming engine, and it is notable that the various experiments with *Coronach* and *Humorist* played an important part in the development of Gresley's later streamlined A4s, four of which were fitted with similar double chimneys when new in 1938. However, the softer exhaust from *Humorist's* double chimney again caused problems with forward vision from the footplate, resulting in further modifications.

T. G. Hepburn

Plate 57: *Left* and 58: *Below* In an attempt to lift the exhaust, the beading was removed from the double chimney, and wing deflector plates were again fitted, but longer than the 1933 variety because of the increased chimney dimensions. These alterations were carried out in February 1938 and were thought to be reasonably successful. In June 1938 *Humorist* is seen after arrival at Kings Cross.

W. B. Greenfield, NELPG Collection

Plate 59: Right Another 1938 picture of *Humorist* with plain double chimney and wing deflectors. It is approaching Potters Bar with the up 'Harrogate Pullman' attached to the GNR eight-wheeled tender which it retained for its entire life. These GNR tenders had a capacity of 8 tons of coal and 5,000 gallons of water.

C. R. L. Coles

Plate 60: Left In May 1947 large smoke deflectors were fitted to *Humorist*, similar to the ones which were fitted to the Peppercorn A2s, and in June 1948 a small beading was fitted to the top of its chimney. It is seen near Potters Bar in 1948 with a down express, having been given its BR number in June 1948.

N. Stead Collection

Plate 61: Right On 14th July 1953 *Humorist* is seen in its final form, still with large smoke deflectors, but with a new lipped chimney of the type fitted to the Peppercorn A1s, which it received in April 1951. It is passing Portobello with a down train whilst allocated to Haymarket.

P. H. Wells

FURTHER DEVELOPMENTS

Plate 62: Left   After the success of the double blastpipe and chimney fitted to *Humorist* in 1937, it is rather surprising that similar improvements were not then carried out to the rest of the class. It was not until 15th May 1958 that authority was given for the remaining A3s to be fitted with double blastpipes and chimneys, as seen on No. 60036 *Colombo* at Neville Hill on 8th March 1961.

G. W. Morrison

Plate 63: Centre   The entire Class had been fitted with double chimneys by January 1960 at an approximate cost of only £150 per engine, and this succeeded in improving the performance of the A3s quite considerably, bearing in mind that by then some were over 35 years of age. Once again, however, there were problems with drifting exhaust obscuring vision from the footplate, and between October and December 1959 four A3s, Nos. 60048/55/61 and 60112, were fitted with small wing deflectors of the type fitted to *Humorist* in 1938 in an attempt to cure the problem. No. 60112 *St. Simon* is seen with these wing deflectors at Grantham on 21st April 1960.

P. H. Groom

Plate 64: Below   These wing deflectors were not thought to be ideal and in October 1960 No. 60049 *Galtee More* was experimentally fitted with German style trough deflectors. These were very successful and in March 1961 authority was given for the A3s to have them fitted as they passed through Works for repairs. Not all the A3s were fitted, as can be seen from the summary, and the appearance of the ones which were fitted with them was certainly not enhanced. No. 60049 is at Doncaster having been altered to left-hand drive in May 1954.

G. W. Morrison

Plate 65: Above No. 60109 *Hermit* was built in 1923, rebuilt as an A3 in 1943, and is seen rejuvenated after receiving a double blastpipe and chimney in March 1959. It is passing Hornsey on 8th May 1959 heading the down 'Talisman'.

P. H. Groom

Plate 66: Below No. 60066 *Merry Hampton* storms through Wood Green about 1955 with a down express. On 26th October 1947 this engine had its cab wrecked when it overturned at Goswick, and in January 1948 it was given the high ventilator cab, visible in this picture, from *St. Simon* (see *Plate 30*).

N. Sprinks

Plate 67: Above   Possibly one of A. C. Cawston's finest pictures shows No. 55 *Woolwinder* passing the much photographed GNR somersault signal at Greenwood whilst heading the 4.00pm Kings Cross–Leeds express on 22nd April 1948. It is resplendent in LNER lined-out green livery, but the numbers and letters are in unshaded yellow Gill Sans style which was first introduced in March 1947.

Plate 68: Opposite Top   In June 1959, shortly after being fitted with a double chimney, No. 60070 *Gladiateur* is passing Potters Bar with a Kings Cross–Leeds express.

D. Cross

Plate 69: Opposite Bottom   No. 60039 *Sandwich* emerges from Welwyn North Tunnel on 29th September 1960 heading a morning Kings Cross–Leeds express. It is in the standard BR Brunswick Green livery with orange and black lining, and has a Diagram 107 A4 boiler. From 1954 these A4-type boilers were fitted to a total of thirty-six A3s at one time or another, as replacement A3 boilers were not then being ordered.

D. Cross

Plate 70: Above   On Saturday 3rd May 1957 No. 60046 *Diamond Jubilee* is working hard past Potters Bar with the 3.52pm Kings Cross–Leeds express.

N. Sprinks

Plate 71: Below   No. 60039 *Sandwich* was one of the last Eastern Region A3s to run with a single chimney, and it is heading a down afternoon express near Finsbury Park on 8th May 1959.

P. H. Groom

Plate 75: Above An up express is approaching Potters Bar about 1956 behind No. 60054 *Prince of Wales*. This engine was built as an A1 in December 1924 and named *Manna* until December 1926.

N. Sprinks

Plate 76: Below No. 60080 *Dick Turpin* has just emerged from the original bore of Hadley Wood South Tunnel at Greenwood with a Leeds–Kings Cross express in June 1959.

D. Cross

Plate 77: *Above*   No. 60109 *Hermit* takes the up slow line at Stoke Summit on 21st July 1962 with the 'White Rose' in order to make way for the 'Queen of Scots' Pullman.

G. W. Morrison

Plate 78: *Below*   In filthy external condition, No. 60046 *Diamond Jubilee* approaches Peterborough with an up express, just before being withdrawn from service, in June 1963, the date when steam was officially banned from working South from Peterborough.

S. C. Crook

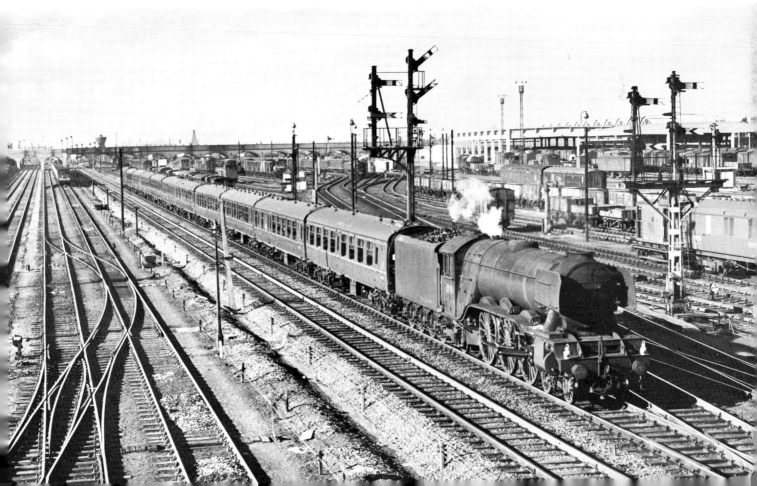

Plate 79: Left The first of three pictures on this page of A3s in rather forlorn condition and approaching the end of their lives. No. 60075 *St. Frusquin* of Gateshead is climbing to Stoke Tunnel past the site of Great Ponton station with an up Newcastle express on 17th June 1961.

G. W. Morrison

Plate 80: Above Another picture taken on Saturday 17th June 1961, this time of No. 60066 *Merry Hampton* of Kings Cross leaving Grantham and starting the climb to Stoke Summit with an up express.

G. W. Morrison

Plate 81: Left Another up departure from Grantham is seen, this time on 5th September 1959, headed by No. 60067 *Ladas* in particularly run-down condition.

G. W. Morrison

Plate 82: Above   Shortly after No. 60048 *Doncaster* had been fitted with a double chimney it is seen accelerating away from Peterborough on 31st July 1959 heading an up express which is formed of a variety of stock including some LMS.

P. H. Groom

Plate 83: Below   No. 60059 *Tracery* of Kings Cross is passing Saltersford, just south of Grantham, on the climb to Stoke Summit, heading a morning Leeds–Kings Cross express. It has just suffered a signal check but has a full head of steam for the remainder of the climb.

T. Boustead

Plates *84* and *85*   Two pictures of East Coast expresses diverted from the East Coast main line because of engineering works. *Above* No. 60109 *Hermit* is leaving Cambridge with an up express on a May Sunday in 1960 and *Below* No. 60092 *Fairway* is passing through Lincoln Central on 1st June 1957, also with an up express.

(Plate 84) *S. C. Crook*, (Plate 85) *J. P. Wilson*

Plate 86: Right Back on the East Coast main line, No. 60065 *Knight of Thistle* is leaving Grantham with the 9.45am Newcastle–Kings Cross express on 19th July 1958.

P. H. Groom

Plate 87: Below The A3s sported a variety of different colours, and with the possible exception of wartime unlined black, looked fine in each. Following the wartime measures, and the reversion to LNER green, No. 60091 *Captain Cuttle* was given an experimental purple livery with yellow lining, in April 1948. The lining was soon amended to cream and red, and it was one of only seven A3s (Nos. 60036/45/71/4/5/84/91) to be given this livery. It is seen in this purple livery leaving Grantham on 7th May 1949 with a down Newcastle express. It was then announced that blue with black and white lining was to be the standard livery, with the lettering 'British Railways' on the tender being replaced by a lion and wheel emblem. This livery appeared in May 1949, and between then and March 1951 all but two A3s (Nos. 60070/6) acquired it. In August 1951 their final BR livery of Brunswick green with orange and black lining appeared, but until about 1957 with varying tender emblems.

J. P. Wilson

Plate 88: Above An afternoon Kings Cross–York train is accelerated away from its Grantham stop by No. 60064 *Tagalie* (named *William Whitelaw* until July 1941, see *Plate 26*) on 20th September 1958.

T. Boustead

Plate 89: Below In BR blue livery, No. 60109 *Hermit*, still with right-hand drive, is leaving Grantham with a Kings Cross slow on 2nd August 1952.

J. P. Wilson

Plate 90: Above   On standby duty at Grantham on 20th July 1963 in case of a diesel failure is No. 60054 *Prince of Wales* in its final form with double chimney and trough deflectors. It is carrying a Diagram 107 A4-type boiler which was fitted in 1958. When these A4-type boilers were fitted to the A3s the working pressure was reduced from 250 lb/sq in to 220 lb/sq in, the same as the ordinary A3 boilers. The dimensions of the A4-type boilers were slightly different, however, with the 'banjo' dome further forward. The arrangement of wash out plugs on the side of the firebox was also slightly different, with the rear one on the side of the firebox further forward and higher up on the Diagram 107 boiler.

T. Boustead

Plate 91: Above   Gresley A1s had worked over the Great Central Section, as seen in Section One, from late 1938 until being transferred away during the war years of 1943/4. Gresley non-streamlined Pacifics returned to the GC Section early in 1949 in the shape of the rebuilt A3s, when six were sent to Leicester and three to Neasden. No. 60104 *Solario*, transferred to Leicester in June 1950, is leaving Aylesbury with the 8.25am Manchester London Road–Marylebone on 2nd November 1953.

N. Sprinks

GREAT CENTRAL INTERLUDE

Plate 92: Below   No. 60052 *Prince Palatine* was transferred to Leicester from Doncaster in May 1949. It is seen passing Haddenham on the former GW and GC joint with the 12.15pm express from Marylebone to Manchester London Road which ran via the High Wycombe route. 23rd April 1952.

A. C. Cawston

Plate 93: Right No. 60107 *Royal Lancer* of Leicester is leaving Chalfont and Latimer on 10th May 1952 with the 1.38pm Marylebone–Woodford Halse stopping train. The third track on the left-hand side is the single track Chesham branch. The engine still has right-hand drive and is in the B R blue livery.
N. Sprinks

Plate 94: Below The 3.20pm Marylebone – Manchester London Road express drifts downhill towards Wendover behind No. 60059 *Tracery*, also a Leicester engine, on 28th February 1953. When the first batch of A3s arrived at Leicester in 1949 they were in very poor shape following several years of wartime neglect. Their performance on the GC was soon improved by the shed staffs, and they quickly became very popular with the crews having plenty of power in reserve for the generally fairly modest loads.
N. Sprinks

Plate 95: Left On Saturday, 6th May 1953, No. 60103 *Flying Scotsman* is seen nearing Culworth Junction, just south of Woodford Halse, heading the 10.25am York–Bournemouth train. *Flying Scotsman* was a Leicester engine and at this period was working the train from Leicester Central to Banbury.

N. Sprinks

Plate 96: Below The 'South Yorkshireman' was one of two titled trains running over the Great Central Section in the early 1950s, the other being the 'Master Cutler'. No. 60107 *Royal Lancer* is climbing from Wendover with the up 'South Yorkshireman', the 10.00am Bradford Exchange–Marylebone, on 28th February 1953. Whilst the A3s were shedded at Leicester and Neasden all heavy repairs had to be done at Colwick and Kings Cross respectively. In the Autumn of 1957 when the London Midland Region was given the responsibility of operating the GC Section all the A3s were once again recalled to the Eastern Region.

N. Sprinks

Plate 97: Above   Because of severe weight restrictions over the Calder Viaduct at Wakefield, Pacific workings from Kings Cross to Leeds did not commence on a regular basis until it had been substantially rebuilt in 1936. The first two A1s (Nos. 2553/5) were transferred to Copley Hill, Leeds, in October 1936 to replace the large-boilered Ivatt Atlantics on the Pullman workings, and from then on A1s/A3s were a common sight inside the terminus at Leeds Central. Here we see No. 60042 *Singapore* waiting to leave on 2nd October 1962 with the up 'White Rose'.   *G. W. Morrison*

Plate 98: Below   Kings Cross A3 No. 60061 *Pretty Polly* is climbing out of Leeds past Beeston heading the 10.00 am Leeds Central–Kings Cross on 25th April 1962.
G. W. Morrison

Plate 99: Left Another Kings Cross engine, No. 60103 *Flying Scotsman*, is about to depart from Leeds Central on 5th June 1961 with the 12.30pm to Kings Cross. Having had a spell at Leicester in the early 1950s, No. 60103 eventually found its way back to Kings Cross in April 1957, after a short spell at Grantham, and it stayed at Kings Cross until being withdrawn from service in January 1963 for private preservation.

G. W. Morrison

Plate 100: Below In particularly shabby condition, No. 60111 *Enterprise* of Grantham is leaving Wakefield Westgate on 24th August 1961 with the Leeds portion of an express from Kings Cross, the Bradford portion having been left at the platform for a Thompson B1 4-6-0 to take it on to Bradford Exchange.

G. W. Morrison

Plate 101: *Above* No. 60046 *Diamond Jubilee* is passing Holbeck High Level on its climb out of Leeds Central with the 11.37 am to Kings Cross on 28th August 1961.

G. W. Morrison

Plate 102: *Below* On 25th April 1962, No. 60066 *Merry Hampton* is just ex-works and on a running-in turn to Doncaster with the 10.10 am Leeds Central–Cleethorpes. From March 1930 all the Gresley Pacifics had been maintained at Doncaster Works, and were until November 1963 when it ceased to repair steam locomotives. For the short period from then until withdrawal of the final A3s, Darlington took over maintenance of them.

G. W. Morrison

A3s WORKING NORTH OF LEEDS

Plate 103: Right In December 1939 Neville Hill MPD, Leeds received its first three A3s (Nos. 2573/80/97) for use on workings from Leeds to Newcastle and Edinburgh. During the war years it lost its allocation of A3s, but they returned shortly after nationalisation. No. 60081 *Shotover* was one of the first Neville Hill A3s, and it was photographed passing Sinderby between Northallerton and Ripon, with a morning Newcastle–Liverpool express via Harrogate in the mid 1950s.

J. W. Hague

Plate 104: Below Another one of the original Neville Hill A3s, No. 60074 *Harvester* is seen shortly after arriving at Leeds City on 15th June 1960 with the 9.55am Newcastle–Liverpool express. The remainder of the journey to Liverpool from Leeds was normally handled by 'Royal Scots', 'Jubilees', 'Patriots' or Stanier Class 5s, and double-heading over the Pennines was a familiar sight.

G. W. Morrison

Plate 105: Right In October 1954 No. 60087 *Blenheim* worked a series of trials over the former Midland Line between Carlisle and Leeds, and although successful, no motive power alterations were made at the time. It was not until Leeds Holbeck MPD had been transferred to the North Eastern Region that A3 Pacifics were moved to there, from February 1960, for services via Ais Gill to Carlisle and Glasgow. They were used very successfully, and a total of nine A3s (60038/69/70/72/77/ 80/82/88/92) were moved to Holbeck during 1960, three from Copley Hill, five from Heaton and one from Gateshead. No. 60082 *Neil Gow* is seen on shed at Holbeck on 6th March 1961 ready to work the down 'Thames-Clyde Express'.

G. W. Morrison

Plate 106: Below No. 60080 *Dick Turpin* is passing under the former GN line at Holbeck Low Level on its way out of Leeds at the head of the down 'Thames-Clyde Express'.

G. W. Morrison

Plate 107: Above   On 16th March 1961 No. 60082 *Neil Gow* is passing Whitehall Junction, shortly after leaving Leeds City, with the down 'Thames-Clyde Express'.

G. W. Morrison

Plate 108: Below   Another picture of the down 'Thames-Clyde Express' leaving Leeds, this time at Wortley Junction on 11th May 1961, with No. 60074 *Harvester* of Neville Hill at the head of the train. In the background another Neville Hill A3, No. 60081 *Shotover*, is waiting to reverse up to Leeds Central to take over the down 'Queen of Scots' Pullman.

G. W. Morrison

Plate 109: Above No. 60069 *Sceptre* only spent a few months at Holbeck, from November 1960 until June 1961, and it is seen at Newlay and Horsforth nearing the end of its journey to Leeds on the up 'Thames-Clyde Express' on 6th June 1961, just before being transferred back to Copley Hill.

G. W. Morrison

Plate 110: Below The down 'Waverley' is leaving Leeds, near Whitehall Junction, on 30th June 1961, behind No. 60072 *Sunstar*.

G. W. Morrison

Plate 111: Above Ais Gill Summit sees an unusual combination on the up 'Thames-Clyde Express' on 16th July 1960. Kingmoor class 5 4-6-0 No. 44886 is piloting Holbeck A3 No. 60038 *Firdaussi*.

G. W. Morrison

Plate 112: Below No. 60038 *Firdaussi* was one of the first two A3s to arrive at Holbeck in February 1960 (the other being No. 60077 *The White Knight*) and it had by far the longest stay, until June 1963, the other eight being transferred away in June and July 1961. It is ready to leave Hellifield with the 10.35 am Leeds–Glasgow on 4th November 1961.

G. W. Morrison

Plate 113: Right The A3s worked over the former G&SWR lines to Glasgow St. Enoch from Carlisle, and No. 60082 *Neil Gow* is about to depart from Carlisle with the down 'Thames-Clyde Express' on 20th August 1960.

G. W. Morrison

Plate 114: Below No. 60077 *The White Knight* has just arrived at Carlisle from Glasgow on the up 'Thames-Clyde Express', and is taking water before departing for Leeds on 13th July 1960.

T. Boustead

Plate 115: Left On 22nd May 1961 No. 60072 *Sunstar* is approaching Kingmoor soon after leaving Carlisle with the down 'Thames-Clyde Express'.

G. W. Morrison

Plate 116: Below The up 'Thames-Clyde Express' leaving Carlisle, near Petteril Bridge Junction, with *Sunstar* in action again, in January 1961. With the exception of No. 60038 *Firdaussi*, the short reign of the A3s at Holbeck ended with the 1961 Summer timetable when Sulzer type 4 diesels were introduced on the Leeds-Glasgow services.

S. C. Crook

Plate 117: Above   No. 60069 *Sceptre* stands at Wortley Junction, Leeds ready for the down 'Queen of Scots' Pullman on 3rd May 1961. Diagram 94HP boiler with round dome, GNR tender.

G. W. Morrison

Plate 118: Above   No. 60100 *Spearmint* at Gateshead MPD on 8th February 1964. Diagram 94A boiler with New Type Non-Corridor tender. This engine was one of the last three A3s to survive into 1965 (60041/52/100), all allocated to St. Margaret's.

G. W. Morrison

Plate 119: Below   No. 60070 *Gladiateur* at Farnley Junction MPD on 16th June 1961. All the Holbeck A3s were given boiler washouts elsewhere, often at Farnley Junction, as their 60' 10⅝" wheelbase prevented them from using the turntables inside the Holbeck roundhouses.

G. W. Morrison

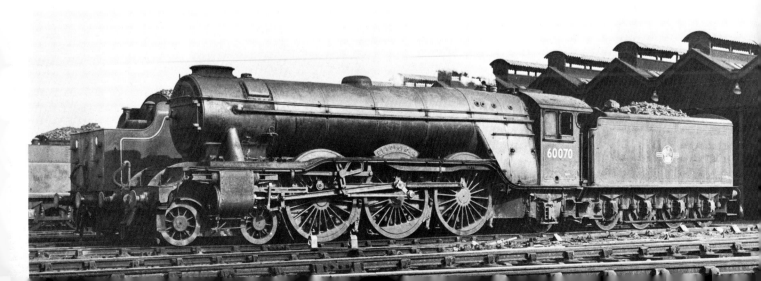

Plate 120: Above On 13th December 1962 No. 60039 *Sandwich* eases off the swing bridge at Selby whilst working an up fitted freight.

J. S. Whiteley

Plate 121: Below No. 60112 *St. Simon* is leaving York on 16th June 1962 with a Kings Cross train. It is still fitted with wing deflectors which it received in December 1959, prior to being fitted with trough deflectors later in 1962.

G. W. Morrison

Plate 122: Above   On the race track north of York. On 10th August 1957 No. 60069 *Sceptre* passes Pilmoor at well over 70mph with the afternoon Newcastle–Birmingham express which at this time was allowed 42 minutes for the 44 miles from Darlington to York.

G. W. Morrison

Plate 123: Below   A down express is hurried north past Benningborough on 6th August 1961 by No. 60064 *Tagalie*.

G. W. Morrison

Plate 124: Above The 1.40pm Carlisle–Edinburgh Waverley is seen in June 1964 behind No. 60052 *Prince Palatine* shortly after leaving Carlisle. It was deputising for a failed diesel on this occasion and subsequently was the last A3 to be withdrawn from service in January 1966.

S. C. Crook

A3s ON THE WAVERLEY ROUTE

Plate 125: Below No. 60057 *Ormonde* is leaving Newcastleton with the midday Edinburgh–Carlisle stopping train on 8th July 1961.

G. W. Morrison

Plate 126: Above   After the A3s had been replaced by diesels on East Coast main line expresses, several were transferred to St. Margaret's for use on the Waverley route. No. 60057 *Ormonde* was one of eleven A3s to be transferred to St. Margaret's from Haymarket between July 1960 and January 1963, and it is seen passing through Galashiels in 1961, whilst still allocated to Haymarket.

N. Stead

Plate 127: Below   In their latter days they were often seen on freight workings, and No. 60040 *Cameronian* is leaving Carlisle with the 16.15 freight from Kingmoor to Millerhill in April 1964. At this time *Cameronian* was allocated to Gateshead and was generally found on freight workings between Newcastle and Edinburgh.

S. C. Crook

Plate 128: Above No. 60042 *Singapore* was one of the A3s which ended its days working from St. Margaret's on freight over the Waverley route, and it is seen approaching Falahill Summit on 9th May 1964 heading a Millerhill–Kingmoor freight.

D. Cross

Plate 129: Below No. 60052 *Prince Palatine* is heading a Kingmoor–Millerhill freight near Gorebridge on 5th September 1963, having just been transferred to St. Margaret's from Gateshead.

D. Cross

Plate 130: Above Throughout its entire life of almost forty years No. 60083 *Sir Hugo* was allocated to the North East, spending over thirty-eight years in two separate spells at Heaton working primarily East Coast expresses. In June 1963, however, it is seen climbing Beattock Bank having rather surprisingly been diagrammed at Kingmoor to work the 10.10am Euston–Perth. At this period ex-LNER engines were often to be found at Carlisle Kingmoor following the closure of Carlisle Canal MPD.

S. C. Crook

Plate 133: Above   Another scene on the former Glasgow and South Western, at Kilmarnock on a wet August day in 1963, with No. 60071 *Tranquil* leaving with a Leeds—Glasgow train.

D. Cross

Plate 134: Below   In June 1962 Nos. 60090/4 were transferred to Glasgow St. Rollox MPD where they stayed until withdrawal in October 1963 and February 1964 respectively. During this period they were used on Glasgow—Aberdeen expresses, and on 2nd March 1963 No. 60090 *Grand Parade* is leaving Dunblane on one such working.

D. Cross

Plate 131: Upper Left   No. 60057 *Ormonde* makes an impressive exit from Mound Tunnel as it leaves Edinburgh Waverley on 3rd September 1957 with an Aberdeen express.

P. H. Groom

Plate 132: Lower Left   One of the Holbeck A3s, No. 60082 *Neil Gow*, is seen on the former Glasgow and South Western line near Garrochburn heading a Glasgow St. Enoch—Leeds train in 1960.

D. Cross

OVERHAUL AT DONCASTER

Plate 135: Left   On 20th March 1960 No. 60103 *Flying Scotsman* is seen in the erecting shop during one of its last overhauls before being privately restored.

G. W. Morrison

Plate 136: Below   In immaculate ex-works condition No. 60085 *Manna* stands outside on 29th April 1962. During this visit to Doncaster its Diagram 107 boiler had been changed for a Diagram 94A boiler, it had been given a GNR tender for the first time and trough deflectors had just been fitted.

G. W. Morrison

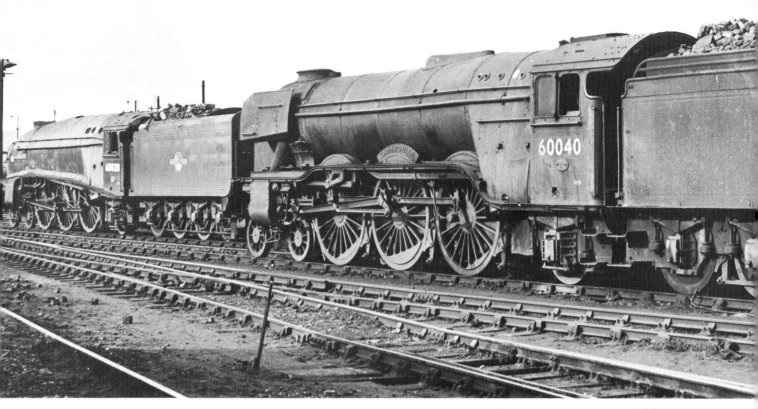

SHED PARTNERS

Plate 137: Above   Gresley Class A4 Pacific No. 60020 *Guillemot* stands alongside No. 60040 *Cameronian* at Doncaster MPD on 24th March 1963.

G. W. Morrison

Plate 138: Below   Converted Royal Scot 4-6-0 No. 46130 *The West Yorkshire Regiment* and No. 60038 *Firdaussi* are being prepared at Leeds Holbeck MPD on 8th March 1961 for the up and down 'Thames-Clyde Express' respectively. Engines were changed at Leeds City on the Anglo-Scottish services, but the Holbeck A3s were always confined to workings North from Leeds.

G. W. Morrison

THEIR FINAL DAYS

Plate 139: Left On 18th April 1964 No. 60051 *Blink Bonny* is near Mirfield with a railtour organised jointly by the Halifax Railfans Club and Gresley Society from Huddersfield to Derby and Crewe. *Blink Bonny* was withdrawn from service in November 1964 having given forty years' faithful service.

J. S. Whiteley

Plates 140 and *141: Above* and *Left* A sickening sight at Bathgate on 31st March 1964 for any Gresley enthusiast. Nos. 60057 *Ormonde* and 60099 *Call Boy* were both withdrawn from service at St. Margaret's MPD in October 1963, and can be seen awaiting the cutter's torch, the nameplates and makers' plates having been removed for safe keeping, and no doubt now lovingly cherished by an enthusiast. No. 60104 *Solario* was the first A3 to be withdrawn, in December 1959, with six more going in 1961, twelve in 1962, thirty-three in 1963, twenty-three in 1964, two in 1965, and the last one No. 60052 *Prince Palatine* in January 1966, their memory perpetuated by No. 4472 *Flying Scotsman* restored in working order.

G. W. Morrison

THOMPSON CLASS A2/2

Original No.	First 1946 No.	Second 1946 No.		BR No.		Name	Built as P2 Doncaster	Works No.	Rebuilt Doncaster	Withdrawn
2001		501	8/46	60501	5/48	Cock o' the North	5/1934	1789	9/44	2/60
2002		502	5/46	60502	7/48	Earl Marischal	10/1934	1796	6/44	7/61
2003		503	6/46	60503	9/48	Lord President	6/1936	1836	12/44	11/59
2004		504	6/46	60504	3/48	Mons Meg	7/1936	1839	11/44	1/61
2005	994 4/46	505	5/46	60505	6/48	Thane of Fife	8/1936	1840	1/43	11/59
2006		506	6/46	60506	12/48	Wolf of Badenoch	9/1936	1842	5/44	4/61

When Edward Thompson succeeded Sir Nigel Gresley in April 1941 as Chief Mechanical Engineer of the LNER, he was confronted with an immediate need for standardisation of designs and simplification of maintenance procedures because of the difficult wartime conditions then prevailing.

Amongst his first proposals was a new Pacific design with 6 feet 2 inches driving wheels, three 18½ inches diameter cylinders and an A4 boiler. In essence it was a mixed traffic version of Gresley's Class A4 without the streamlined casing, but in the event he first chose to rebuild the six Gresley three-cylinder Class P2 2-8-2s as Pacifics. These P2s had been designed by Gresley for working over the difficult line between Edinburgh and Aberdeen, the first two of which, Nos. 2001 and 2002, were built at Doncaster in 1934. These two were followed by four more from Doncaster in 1936, Nos. 2003-6, which although mechanically similar to the first two, had streamlined front ends similar to the A4 Pacifics. Nos. 2001 and 2002 were first rebuilt in 1938 and 1936 respectively when they too were given streamlined casings at the front.

In April 1942 drawings were prepared for rebuilding the P2s showing the pony truck and the leading pair of coupled wheels replaced by a bogie, and the streamlined casing removed. Thompson was determined to make full use of existing parts wherever possible, and the rather short outside connecting rods were therefore retained resulting in the bogie being positioned in front of the 20 inches diameter outside cylinders. Three independent sets of motion replaced Gresley's derived valve gear, a lengthy smokebox was incorporated in the design, and a Kylchap arrangement of double blastpipe and chimney was fitted with small wing-type deflectors to help smoke lifting. No. 2005 was the first P2 to be rebuilt in this manner, and it was completed at Doncaster in January 1943. After it had been rebuilt it was first known simply as Class A, but on 27th April 1943 Thompson amended this to Class A2. The other five P2s were rebuilt at Doncaster and were all completed between May and December 1944. On 22nd August 1945 Thompson further amended the classification to A2/2, leaving the classification A2 free for his new standard Pacifics.

After rebuilding they all returned to Scotland to work once again between Edinburgh and Aberdeen, but in 1949 all six were brought South and allocated to York and New England, two making very brief visits to Neville Hill towards the end of 1950. The Class A2/2s were probably the least successful of Thompson's Pacific designs, and it was almost inevitable that they would suffer early withdrawal after a rather undistinguished career. Two were withdrawn late in 1959, one early in 1960 and the other three during 1961.

Plate 142: Below   No. 60506 *Wolf of Badenoch* is on shed at Kings Cross on 14th September 1958.

G. W. Morrison

Plate 143: Above   A look at the original Gresley engines from which Thompson's A2/2s were rebuilt. No. 2001 *Cock o' the North* is seen as originally built at Doncaster in May 1934. It had a double chimney, 6 feet 2 inches eight-coupled wheels and three cylinders with Lentz rotary cam operated poppet valves. No. 2001 was attached to a 5,000 gallon New Type non-corridor tender and was fitted with an ACF1 feed water heater. Later in 1934, in October, the second P2 2-8-2 No. 2002 *Earl Marischal* was completed which was similar in appearance to No. 2001, but differed in the fact that it was not fitted with a feed water heater and was given Gresley's conventional conjugated valve gear. As a result No. 2002 was classified P2/2 and No. 2001 P2/1.

Courtesy National Railway Museum

Plate 144: Below   No. 2003 *Lord President* was one of four more P2s (Nos. 2003–6) which were built in 1936 at Doncaster, and it is seen leaving Edinburgh Waverley in August 1938 with the Aberdeen portion of the down 'Flying Scotsman'. These last four were also classified P2/2, and although they were mechanically similar to No. 2002, their appearance differed considerably in as much as they were built with a wedge-shaped nose similar to Gresley's streamlined A4s. No. 2002 underwent its first rebuilding in 1936 when it was rebuilt to conform with Nos. 2003–6 and No. 2001 was similarly dealt with in April 1938.

A. C. Cawston

Plate 145: Above   No. 2005 *Thane of Fife* was the first P2/2 to be rebuilt by Thompson, and it emerged from Doncaster in January 1943 as a rather unattractive Pacific. The eight-coupled wheel arrangement of the P2s had not proved ideal for the curving line between Edinburgh and Aberdeen, but six of the 6 feet 2 inches diameter driving wheels of the P2s were retained during rebuilding. The original P2 boilers were retained (Diagram 106A on Nos. 2001, 2003–6, and Diagram 108A on No. 2002 which had been switched from No. 2006), but the 20 inches diameter cylinders were positioned behind the front bogie. The original classification after rebuilding was A, but this was soon amended to A2, being further amended to A2/2 in August 1945. No. 2006 is seen after being rebuilt at Doncaster in May 1944 without its nameplates which were refitted in June 1944.

Courtesy National Railway Museum

Plate 146: Below   *Cock o' the North* is seen with its BR number at Grantham on 23rd August 1952. When the P2s were rebuilt their original double chimney arrangement (with the exception of No. 2005 which had a single chimney) was not retained, and they were fitted with the Kylchap double blastpipe arrangement of the type fitted to *Humorist* (see *Plates 56–58*), but with plain straight-sided chimneys.

J. P. Wilson

Plate 147: Above On 17th August 1960 No. 60506 *Wolf of Badenoch* is passing Hadley Wood with a Kings Cross—Newcastle express. During 1951 and 1952 Nos. 60501/2/5/6 were fitted with Diagram 118 boilers, with modifications, of the type fitted to the Peppercorn Pacifics.

D. Cross

Plate 148: Below No. 60503 *Lord President* is seen unusually at the head of the up 'Flying Scotsman' passing Essendine on 3rd September 1955, no doubt deputising for a failed Gresley Pacific. From the early 1950s the A2/2s (with the exception of No. 60506) were fitted with lipped chimneys.

P. H. Wells

A2/2s AT WORK

Plate 149: Above After the A2/2s had been moved from Scotland following the introduction of the Peppercorn Pacifics, they were rarely used on front line work, and were often seen on freight and parcels traffic. No. 60505 *Thane of Fife* was transferred from Haymarket to New England in December 1949, and is passing Essendine on 29th May 1951 heading an up parcels train.

P. H. Wells

Plate 150: Below No. 60504 *Mons Meg* was also transferred from Haymarket to New England in January 1950, and was to spend the rest of its life there until withdrawal in January 1961. It is climbing past Little Ponton towards Stoke Tunnel on 10th June 1950 with a Leeds–Kings Cross train.

J. P. Wilson

Plate 151: Left   Immediately after rebuilding all the A2/2s returned to Scotland for service between Edinburgh and Aberdeen. No. 60505 *Thane of Fife* went to Dundee for a short period and then to Haymarket in April 1943, before being transferred to New England. It is seen on 29th May 1949 at Aberdeen in LNER apple green livery. When the A2/2s appeared they were given unlined black livery, but from 1946 they were all given LNER livery until being changed to Brunswick green from February 1950.

G. W. Sharpe Collection

Plate 152: Below   *Thane of Fife* is seen again, this time in BR livery leaving York with an up Newcastle train. This was the only A2/2 to be given a Diagram 117 boiler (as originally fitted to Thompson's A2/3s) which was fitted with a dummy 'banjo' dome.

G. W. Morrison

Plate 153: Below   No. 60501 *Cock o' the North* is in a forlorn state at Doncaster on 20th March 1960 awaiting scrap, having been withdrawn from service at York in February. The authorities had obviously not foreseen in 1960 just how valuable the plates were to become as collectors' items.

G. W. Morrison

THOMPSON CLASS A2/1

Original No.	Intended V2 No.	Second 1946 No.		BR No.		Name	Date Named	Built Darlington	Works No.	8-Wheel Tender	Withdrawn
3696	(884)	507	5/46	60507	11/48	Highland Chieftain	5/47	5/1944	1930	12/45	12/60
3697	(885)	508	7/46	60508	5/48	Duke of Rothesay	1/47	6/1944	1933	6/49	2/61
3698	(886)	509	5/46	60509	8/48	Waverley	10/46	11/1944	1944	10/46	8/60
3699	(887)	510	6/46	60510	4/48	Robert the Bruce	4/48	1/1945	1950	9/49	11/60

As soon as Thompson had rebuilt class P2 No. 2005 as a Pacific he prepared drawings for his second Pacific. At the time Darlington Works had an order for the final four Class V2 2-6-2s, but in August 1943 authority was given for Pacifics to be built instead of the 2-6-2s. No. 3696 was the first to be completed in May 1944 and it was initially known as Class A, as the first A2/2 had been before it was reclassified, but when the second engine was completed in June 1944 they were reclassified A2/1. The final two engines of the class appeared in November 1944 and January 1945.

The four Thompson Class A2/1s were similar to his earlier A2/2s having the same lengthy smokebox, double blastpipe and chimney, wing-type smoke deflectors, bogie ahead of the outside cylinders, similar valve gear and 6 feet 2 inches coupled wheels. The boilers, however, were of the V2 type with the working pressure increased from 220lb/sq in to 225lb/sq in. The V-shaped cabs were also similar to those of the V2s, and the engines were paired with six-wheel tenders

with a capacity of 4,200 gallons and 7½ tons of coal. These tenders were soon found to have insufficient capacity and by September 1949 all four engines had been given larger eight-wheel tenders with a capacity of 5,000 gallons of water and 9 tons of coal. The only other noticeable change to the appearance of the A2/1s during their life was the fitting of larger smoke deflectors similar to the ones which were fitted to Thompson's later Class A2/3 Pacifics. This was done between October 1946 and April 1948, enabling the fitting of Scottish flavoured nameplates.

All four A2/1s were allocated to Darlington after they were built where they were used on secondary duties. Two were soon transferred to Kings Cross and the other two, Nos. 3698/9, went to Scotland where they remained for the rest of their working lives, being joined by No. 60507 from Kings Cross in December 1949. The A2/1s also suffered early withdrawal, the last one disappearing from service in February 1961.

Plate 154: Below All four A2/1s appeared in wartime unlined black livery with only NE on the tenders. Apart from No. 3697, they were all fitted with electric lighting equipment, between March and July 1945, and in this picture of No. 3698 the alternator which was driven by the rear bogie axle can clearly be seen together with some of the wiring to the lamps. The equipment was removed from all three engines between 1950 and 1952.

Courtesy National Railway Museum

Plate 155: Left All four engines were given their new numbers, between May and July 1946, and No. 508 is seen at Grantham on 20th September 1947, having been named *Duke of Rothesay* in January 1947. Under the liberal coating of post-war filth the engine is still in black livery. A decision was taken in 1946 to replace their wing deflectors with large smoke deflectors similar to the ones which Thompson had used on his A2/3s, but the last one (No. 60510) did not receive them until April 1948.

J. P. Wilson

Plate 156: Above No. 60508 *Duke of Rothesay* is leaving Grantham on a heavy Leeds–Kings Cross express on 17th June 1948. No. 60508 was the only A2/1 never to be allocated in Scotland and spent most of its time until 1950 at Kings Cross working mainly to York and Leeds.

J. P. Wilson

Plate 157: Left The original six-wheel tenders were changed for larger tenders, and No. 60510 *Robert the Bruce* eventually received its brand new tender in September 1949. It is seen passing Melrose on a Waverley route express in the early 1950s, whilst allocated to Haymarket. Nos. 60510 and 60507 were never given LNER green livery, unlike the other two A2/1s, but went straight from black to BR Brunswick green livery in 1949.

N. Stead

Plate 158: Above No. 60507 *Highland Chieftain* on shed at Haymarket on 15th July 1953. Only three new eight-wheel tenders were built for the four A2/1s, *Highland Chieftain* being given the reconditioned tender from Class A4 No. 4469 *Sir Ralph Wedgwood* which was withdrawn in 1942 following air raid damage. This streamlined non-corridor tender was changed from vacuum to steam brake and was attached in December 1945.

P. H. Wells

Plate 159: Below A Kings Cross—Newcastle express is crossing Durham Viaduct in the 1950s behind No. 60508 *Duke of Rothesay*.

N. Stead Collection

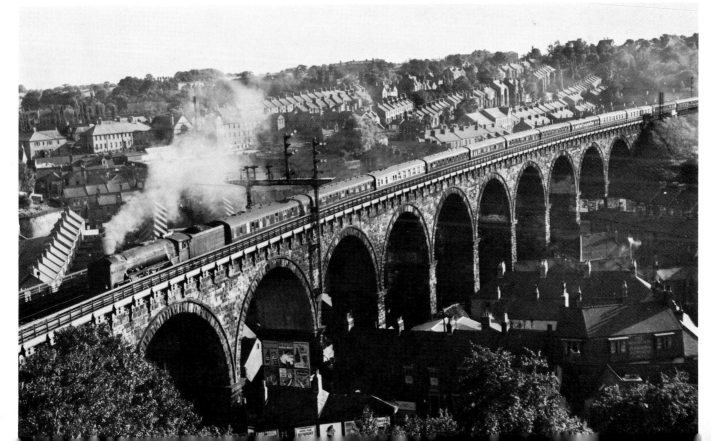

Plate 160: Above In LNER apple green livery, No. 60509 *Waverley* is leaving Aberdeen with an Edinburgh express on 28th August 1949. At this time it was allocated to Haymarket where it spent most of its working life until being withdrawn in August 1960.

J. P. Wilson

Plate 161: Below A scene at Kings Cross in 1952 with No. 60508 *Duke of Rothesay* leaving with the down 'Junior Scotsman' and Class B17/1 No. 61625 *Raby Castle* arriving with a Cambridge train. From June 1950 until withdrawal in February 1961 No. 60508 was allocated to New England participating primarily in secondary duties with the A2/2s.

C. R. L. Coles

THOMPSON CLASS A1/1

First No.	First 1946 No.	Second 1946 No.		BR No.		Name	Built as Gresley A1 Doncaster	Rebuilt Doncaster	Withdrawn
4470	(500)	113	10/46	60113	10/48	Great Northern	4/1922	9/45	11/62

When Gresley's first A1 Pacific No. 1470 *Great Northern* appeared in 1922 it was inconceivable what a controversial engine this was to be. Apart from a very short spell at Gorton during 1944, *Great Northern* had been allocated to Doncaster and Kings Cross participating in duties over the East Coast main line. Its fate was sealed, however, in the summer of 1944 when Thompson produced two drawings of a Gresley Pacific with three separate sets of Walschaerts valve gear to replace the conjugated valve gear. It was the second drawing which was proceeded with, and this showed a 250lb/sq in A4 boiler with 'banjo' dome, the outside cylinders set well back behind the bogie and shortened cab sides. Despite the efforts of several colleagues and officials, and to the horror of Gresley admirers, Thompson chose to rebuild Gresley's pioneer Pacific *Great Northern* in this manner. Although some would suggest that this was simply a tactless move on Thompson's part, the general feeling was, and probably still is, that it was a quite intentional and somewhat vindictive act. It was possibly motivated by a feeling of inferiority in following the great Sir Nigel Gresley, aggravated by the frustration of wartime conditions.

During rebuilding very little of the original Gresley engine was retained, and when *Great Northern* reappeared in September 1945 it was given a unique royal blue livery. It was paired with the new type non-corridor tender which had been fitted in February 1937, and although it was originally proposed to fit wing-type smoke deflectors similar to those fitted to the A2/2s and A2/1s, in the event it emerged from Doncaster without deflectors. However, during its first light repair in December 1945 large smoke deflectors were fitted and the nameplates were transferred to these from the sides of the smokebox.

It is worthy of note that Thompson intended to similarly rebuild all the remaining Gresley Pacifics of 180lb/sq in boiler pressure which by then had been reclassified A10, but thankfully no further rebuilding took place.

Great Northern was still classified A1 after rebuilding, but in January 1947 it was reclassified A1/1 to make way for the new Peppercorn Pacifics which are dealt with in Sections 8 and 9. After being rebuilt it was allocated to Kings Cross after some trial running from Doncaster, but it was rarely in the limelight and suffered considerable teething troubles. In 1947 it was used on trial running at Gateshead and Haymarket, but soon returned to Kings Cross. It subsequently had spells at New England, Grantham and Doncaster, invariably being used on secondary duties due to its unreliability. However, to be fair, *Great Northern* performed better after being rebuilt than it did as an A1 Pacific and was sometimes capable of producing a better performance than a single chimney A3 or A4. As a non-standard engine early withdrawal was inevitable and on 19th November 1962 it was condemned with a badly worn middle cylinder.

Plate 162: Below   Great Northern at Doncaster Works in September 1945 immediately after being rebuilt. It is in blue livery with red lining, in itself very attractive, but the overall appearance of this somewhat ungainly Pacific was certainly not enhanced by the original short cab sides which were soon altered.

Courtesy National Railway Museum

Plate 163: Above   This picture taken in December 1945 clearly shows the first modifications to *Great Northern*, the fitting of large smoke deflectors and the lengthened cab sides. It is still in its unique blue livery, and the axle driven alternator on the rear bogie axle can be seen which provided electric lighting in the same manner as fitted to three A2/1s. The Kylchap double blastpipe and beaded stovepipe chimney which was fitted on rebuilding can also be seen in this picture.

Courtesy National Railway Museum

Plate 164: Below   On 30th October 1948 *Great Northern* is approaching Grantham with the down 'Queen of Scots' Pullman. It was initially allocated the number 500 (which was subsequently given to the first of Thompson's new standard Pacifics, see Section 7), but after the scheme for renumbering the Pacifics was altered in 1946 it was given the number 113, following a decision to add it to the end of the numbers allocated to the Gresley Pacifics. In May 1947 it emerged from Doncaster Works in LNER apple green livery, following its first general repair. When it emerged from its next general repair, in October 1948, it was still in LNER green but had 'British Railways' on the tender and had been given its BR number. The axle driven alternator for the Metropolitan Vickers electric lighting was replaced by a Stones steam driven generator in May 1947 which was positioned behind one of the smoke deflectors, but the complete electric lighting equipment was removed in April 1951.

J. P. Wilson

Plate 165: Right Great Northern participated in main line workings at Kings Cross, together with other classes of Pacific, after being moved back following some trials in Scotland and the North East. In June 1950 it was transferred to New England for secondary duties, and in September 1951 it was sent to Grantham along with some Peppercorn A1s to replace some A4s and A3s which had been transferred to Kings Cross. Whilst at Grantham until September 1957 it was often kept as spare engine, but on 13th June 1957 it is emerging from Wood Green Tunnel with a down Newcastle express.

P. H. Groom

Plate 166: Below It had been given its Brunswick green livery in August 1952 following a short spell in BR blue, from January 1950. In May 1951 new nameplates incorporating the GNR crest had been fitted, and the beaded stovepipe chimney was replaced by a lipped chimney. In September 1957 *Great Northern* returned to Kings Cross, but after only a few weeks it was transferred to Doncaster where it is seen on 18th October 1959.

N. Stead

Plate 167: Left On 24th July 1962 *Great Northern* is seen on the race track north of York, near Benningborough, heading a Kings Cross–Newcastle express.

G. W. Morrison

Plate 168: Below Whilst it was at Doncaster from October 1957 until withdrawal in November 1962 it was generally used on secondary main line duties, and on 9th August 1961 it is leaving Leeds Central on the 2.05 pm stopping train to Doncaster.

G. W. Morrison

THOMPSON CLASS A2/3

Original No.	BR No.		Name	Built	Maker	Works No.	Withdrawn
500	60500	10/49	Edward Thompson	5/1946	Doncaster	2000	6/63
511	60511	4/48	Airborne	7/1946	Doncaster	2002	11/62
512	60512	3/48	Steady Aim	8/1946	Doncaster	2003	6/65
513	60513	11/48	Dante	8/1946	Doncaster	2004	4/63
514	60514	3/48	Chamossaire	9/1946	Doncaster	2005	12/62
515	60515	6/48	Sun Stream	10/1946	Doncaster	2006	11/62
516	60516	10/48	Hycilla	11/1946	Doncaster	2007	11/62
517	60517	8/48	Ocean Swell	11/1946	Doncaster	2008	11/62
518	60518	7/48	Tehran	12/1946	Doncaster	2009	11/62
519	60519	10/48	Honeyway	2/1947	Doncaster	2010	12/62
520	60520	8/48	Owen Tudor	3/1947	Doncaster	2011	6/63
521	60521	5/48	Watling Street	5/1947	Doncaster	2012	11/62
522	60522	9/49	Straight Deal	6/1947	Doncaster	2013	6/65
523	60523	7/49	Sun Castle	8/1947	Doncaster	2014	6/63
524	60524	1/49	Herringbone	9/1947	Doncaster	2015	2/65

Thompson's fourth class of Pacific to appear was not a rebuild of an earlier engine, but was his new 6 feet 2 inches standard design. Fifteen were built in 1946/7, and they were his final series of A2s. This standard class was largely based on his earlier A2/2s, but the boiler pressure was raised from 225lb/sq in to 250lb/sq in, and the diameter of the three cylinders was reduced from 20 inches to 19 inches.

No. 500 was the first of these new standard Pacifics, completed at Doncaster Works in May 1946, and it was the 2,000th engine built there since construction commenced in 1867. It was named *Edward Thompson* a few days after entering service in honour of its designer who was retiring as Chief Mechanical Engineer of the LNER in June 1946 at the age of 65. The first ten engines, Nos. 500, 511–519, were classified A2, but from April 1947 they were given the classification A2/3 to make way for Peppercorn's modified design described in Section 8. Nos. 520–524 were completed during the final year of the LNER and were classified A2/3 from new. All fifteen engines were turned out in full LNER green livery and had large smoke deflectors, although at one time it was intended to fit them with small wing-type deflectors, similar to the ones fitted to the A2/2s.

After the first engine had undergone some trials at Gateshead, the majority of the class were then allocated to the North Eastern Area, with four more at Kings Cross and one at Haymarket. In this immediate post-war period a lot of the older Pacifics were in rather run down condition, with the result that the A2/3s were soon at the forefront of main line workings, and continued to be so until the advent of dieselisation. In the early 1960s dieselisation progressed, and twelve had disappeared by early 1963. The last three, Nos. 60512/22/24, lingered on for a while in Scotland, and were all finally withdrawn by June 1965.

Plate 169: Right No. 500 was the first of Thompson's new standard Pacifics and it was named after its designer at an official ceremony at Marylebone station on 31st May 1946. It is seen on 29th May 1946 at Nottingham Victoria with its nameplates covered, en route to London for the naming ceremony. The initial classification A2 is visible on the buffer beam.

J. P. Wilson

Plate 170: Below   No. 500 *Edward Thompson* poses for its official photograph at Doncaster shortly after being completed. Thompson's fifteen new standard Pacifics were similar in many respects to his earlier rebuilds having 6 feet 2 inches driving wheels, outside cylinders positioned behind the bogie and a Diagram 117 boiler similar to the Diagram 106A boiler fitted to the rebuilt P2s, but with the pressure increased to 250lb/sq in. The double blastpipe and chimney arrangement was also similar to his earlier Pacifics, but these final engines were fitted with large smoke deflectors which certainly helped to improve their appearance. Although these fifteen engines were initially allocated the numbers 200–214, in April 1946 the Pacific renumbering scheme was altered and all the various A2s were numbered in the 500 series. The first standard Pacific was given the number 500 and the remaining fourteen were numbered 511–524, following the A2/2s and A2/1s. They were all turned out from Doncaster in full LNER lined green livery, and Nos. 511–524 were all named after racehorses from new.

Courtesy National Railway Museum

Plate 171: Below   On 9th April 1955 No. 60500 *Edward Thompson* is passing Holbeck High Level as it climbs out of Leeds with the 5.00pm to Kings Cross. In common with several other A2/3s, No. 60500 was transferred to New England from Kings Cross after the introduction of Peppercorn A1s, and from there was used on their main line diagrams.

J. P. Wilson

A2/3s IN SERVICE

Plate 172: Above   BR Brunswick green livery with orange and black lining was adopted on the A2/3s from July 1949, replacing their LNER green livery. With the exception of Nos. 60514/19, all the A2/3s were given lipped chimneys from 1951 which replaced their original beaded stovepipe chimneys. No. 60500 *Edward Thompson* is seen at York on 5th October 1962. The Metro-Vick electric lighting equipment which was fitted when new was removed in the early 1950s.

G. W. Morrison

Plate 173: Below   In April 1961 No. 60512 *Steady Aim* of York was one of nine A2/3s shedded in the North Eastern Region, six at York and three at Heaton. They covered a variety of East Coast duties, but were not often seen on the Waverley route as seen here leaving Carlisle on the 9.20am to Edinburgh.

S. C. Crook

Plate 174: Left No. 60513 *Dante* of New England is approaching Pilmoor on 18th June 1961 with the down 'Heart of Midlothian', a regular turn for an A2/3.

G. W. Morrison

Plate 175: Below Throughout its life No. 60517 *Ocean Swell* was only moved once, in October 1961 from Heaton to Tweedmouth. It is seen leaving Grantham on 20th September 1958 with a Kings Cross—Newcastle express.

T. Boustead

Plate 176: Above No. 60513 *Dante* is seen heading the down 'Heart of Midlothian' at Potters Bar in 1954 during rebuilding work. This was the first A2/3 to be given a Diagram 118 boiler with 'banjo' dome, in August 1950, which were fitted to the Peppercorn Pacifics, and which were interchangeable with their original Diagram 117 boilers.

M. W. Earley

Plate 177: Right The up 'Northumbrian' emerges from Hadley Wood South Tunnel at Greenwood on 5th June 1950 behind No. 60517 *Ocean Swell* of Heaton, newly painted in its Brunswick green livery.

A. C. Cawston

Plates 178 and *179*   Two views of No. 60512 *Steady Aim* awaiting repair at Doncaster Works on 3rd March 1963. The Diagram 118 boilers, seen here, were of the type fitted to the Peppercorn Pacifics and were slightly lighter than the Diagram 117 boilers which were fitted to the A2/3s when built. No spare boilers had been built for the A2/3s, and after it was decided that they were interchangeable with the Diagram 118 type, all the class received one at some time. The tenders fitted to the A2/3s were based on the streamlined non-corridor tenders of the 1936 variety, but when they were built, snap-headed rivets were used instead of countersunk rivets. Doncaster was responsible for maintenance of the A2/3s until it ceased to repair steam locomotives late in 1963.

G. W. Morrison

Plate 180: Above   Not a very taxing load for No. 60520 *Owen Tudor* as it returns to Doncaster on the 2.05 pm local from Leeds Central on 28th June 1961.

G. W. Morrison

Plate 181: Below   No. 60518 *Tehran* heads an up express, formed of a variety of stock, near East Markham on 30th March 1959.

T. Boustead

Plate 182: Above In November 1962 the North Eastern Region withdrew Nos. 60512/15/16/18/22/24 from service at York. In view of the fact, however, that Nos. 60512/22/24 had only just undergone heavy repairs, these three received a stay of execution and were transferred to the Scottish Region in exchange for No. 60519 and two Peppercorn A2s (Nos. 60531/36) which were transferred on paper to York and immediately condemned. Nos. 60512/24 went to St. Margaret's but soon joined No. 60522 at Polmadie. No. 60524 *Herringbone* is passing Gretna Green, on the former G&SWR, with the Sundays only 12.30pm Carlisle–Glasgow parcels in April 1964.

S. C. Crook

Plate 183: Below *Herringbone* had a spell at Aberdeen, from December 1962 until September 1963, and is seen on 30th May 1963 heading the Aberdeen portion of the up West Coast Postal near Craigenhill Summit, not far from Carstairs.

D. Cross

Plate 184: Right In June 1963 the remaining A2/3s in the Southern Area (Nos. 60500/20/23, all at New England) were withdrawn, leaving the three Scottish survivors. By September 1963 all these three were at Polmadie where they were used rather infrequently on secondary duties. No. 60524 *Herringbone* was the first of the three to be withdrawn, in February 1965, and it is seen nearing South Lanark Junction, just north of Carstairs, on 9th May 1964 heading the early morning Lockerbie–Glasgow stopping train. This was a Kingmoor working, often a 'Jubilee' or 'Britannia' and No. 60524 was probably deputising for a failure.

Plate 185: Below No. 60522 *Straight Deal* is heading a fitted freight from Kilmarnock to Brent on 15th September 1964 near Garrochburn Sidings, south of Kilmarnock. In their latter days they were often used on freight traffic, and Nos. 60512/22 were the last of all the Thompson Pacifics in service, and were finally withdrawn in June 1965.   *Both D. Cross*

PEPPERCORN CLASS A2

Original No.	BR No.		Name	Built	Maker	Works No.	Double Chimney Fitted	Withdrawn
525	60525	8/49	A. H. Peppercorn	12/1947	Doncaster	2016	–	3/63
526	60526	8/48	Sugar Palm	1/1948	Doncaster	2017	10/49	11/62
E527	60527	6/48	Sun Chariot	1/1948	Doncaster	2018	–	4/65
E528	60528	6/48	Tudor Minstrel	2/1948	Doncaster	2019	–	6/66
E529	60529	9/49	Pearl Diver	2/1948	Doncaster	2020	9/49	12/62
E530	60530	11/48	Sayajirao	3/1948	Doncaster	2021	–	11/66
E531	60531	11/48	Bahram	3/1948	Doncaster	2022	–	12/62
–	60532	When new	Blue Peter	3/1948	Doncaster	2023	9/49	12/66
–	60533	When new	Happy Knight	4/1948	Doncaster	2024	12/49	6/63
–	60534	When new	Irish Elegance	4/1948	Doncaster	2025	–	12/62
–	60535	When new	Hornets Beauty	5/1948	Doncaster	2026	–	6/65
–	60536	When new	Trimbush	5/1948	Doncaster	2027	–	12/62
–	60537	When new	Bachelors Button	6/1948	Doncaster	2028	–	12/62
–	60538	When new	Velocity	6/1948	Doncaster	2029	10/49	11/62
–	60539	When new	Bronzino	8/1948	Doncaster	2030	When built	11/62

In 1944 the construction of thirty new standard 6 feet 2 inches Pacifics had been authorised, and Thompson had intended that these should be to the same basic design as No. 500 (initially class A2 but later reclassified A2/3 as described in Section 7). However, when he was succeeded by Arthur Henry Peppercorn on his retirement in June 1946, it was decided that after the initial batch of fifteen Thompson A2s had been completed, the remaining fifteen engines on order would be built to Peppercorn's improved design. This showed the outside cylinders conventionally positioned astride the bogie, but retained some Thompson features including double chimney and boiler with round dome. However, the original drawings continued to be amended, and by February 1947 Peppercorn decided to fit a boiler with a 'banjo' dome and perforated steam collector, and rather surprisingly revert back to a single chimney arrangement.

Peppercorn's A2 Pacifics were started as soon as the last of Thompson's Pacifics had been completed, and the first one, No. 525 which was named *A. H. Peppercorn*, appeared in December 1947, the last month of the LNER. The first two engines, Nos. 525 and 526, were the only ones to carry the lettering LNER on the tender sides, the remaining thirteen all being lettered British Railways, as they were completed in 1948. Prior to nationalisation twenty more A2s were on order at Doncaster, but this order was cancelled on 4th May 1948.

The decision to fit single chimneys to the A2s was questioned during construction, and at the eleventh hour the last engine, No. 60539, was fitted with a Kylchap double blastpipe and chimney. During 1949 five more A2s were fitted with double chimneys, and these engines were also given MLS multiple valve regulators.

The A2s shared in main line workings with the Gresley and Thompson engines, but because of dieselisation were destined to have a short life, with all the engines shedded in England disappearing by June 1963. The last three Scottish engines survived until 1966, and one of these, No. 60532 *Blue Peter*, has been privately restored in its original LNER apple green livery, but incorrectly lettered LNER on the sides of the tender.

Plate 186: Left Even before Edward Thompson retired, in June 1946, there were proposals in the drawing office to amend the design of his standard Pacifics which were then under construction. The first outline drawing actually appeared during the month Thompson retired, and the immediate difference was a reversion to the orthodox position of the outside cylinders astride the bogie. The three 19″ x 26″ Thompson cylinder arrangement was retained together with Walschaerts valve gear. The Thompson Diagram 117 250lb/sq in boiler was redesigned in November 1946 incorporating a 'banjo' dome and perforated steam collector instead of the round dome, and this new Diagram 118 boiler weighed 7cwt less. The 6 feet 2 inches coupled driving wheels were retained, but rather surprisingly a single chimney was preferred to the Kylchap double blastpipe and chimney arrangement, a decision which was apparently later regretted. The first of Peppercorn's A2s is seen in the paint shop at Doncaster about November 1947. All fifteen engines were given LNER green livery, but only the first two ever carried the lettering LNER on the tender, although only No. 525 in fact appeared before Nationalisation.
Courtesy National Railway Museum

Plate 187: Above Before they were given their BR numbers, Nos. 527–531 were given the prefix E, and on 24th April 1948 No. E530 *Sayajirao* is seen on the turntable at Grantham, when barely one month old. In their early days, all the A2s carried electric lighting equipment, as can be seen in this picture, but in later years it was generally either out of use or removed. All the A2s were named when new, and with the exception of the first one, all were named after racehorses.

J. P. Wilson

Plate 188: Below No. 60533 *Happy Knight* is passing Greenwood on 29th July 1948 with the down 'Yorkshire Pullman'. No. 60533 was initially allocated to New England but was soon transferred to Copley Hill to join Nos. 60536/7. These three stayed there until late 1948/early 1949, and were used on through workings to Kings Cross. No. 60533 spent its entire life shedded in England, and moved sheds on no fewer than twelve separate occasions.

A. C. Cawston

Plate 189: Above   No. 60539 *Bronzino* was unique in being the only Peppercorn A2 to be built with a Kylchap double blastpipe and chimney. It was a last minute decision during construction, and it was fitted with the same type as the A2/3s. The short smokebox, however, was retained and *Bronzino* was therefore not fitted with self-cleaning apparatus as was fitted to all the other A2s. The following year five A2s were fitted with a similar double chimney arrangement, but these were all given MLS multiple valve regulators, and at the same time the self-cleaning apparatus in the smokebox was removed. No. 60539 *Bronzino* is leaving Grantham with the up 'Flying Scotsman' on 7th May 1949. Note the original positioning of the smokebox number plate above the top hinge on the smokebox door, resulting in the top lamp iron having to be raised.

J. P. Wilson

Plate 190: Below   When *Bronzino* was being built it inadvertently received the bogie which was intended for the first of Peppercorn's A1s, No. 60114. This was distinguishable by the two holes in the front stretcher, clearly visible in the upper picture, all the other A2s having a plain front stretcher. This picture of *Bronzino* was taken at Grantham on 5th April 1961 after the more attractive lipped chimney had been fitted. As all the A2s were originally intended to have single chimneys, the smokebox was 1′ 4⅝″ shorter than that of the A2/3s (compare *Plate 170*), and this was not amended when *Bronzino* was fitted with a double chimney, although the self-cleaning apparatus which was fitted to all the A2/3s, was omitted. *Bronzino* was allocated to Heaton when built, and stayed there until October 1961 when it was moved to Tweedmouth, before being withdrawn later the following year.

P. H. Groom

The three pictures on this page illustrate the variations within the class.

Plate 191: Right shows No. 60534 *Irish Elegance* in April 1962. This engine has its original single chimney and the Diagram 118 boiler with 'banjo' dome.

G. W. Morrison

Plate 192: Centre shows No. 60528 *Tudor Minstrel* at Doncaster on 29th April 1962. This was one of the A2s which retained its single chimney, but was one of seven (Nos. 60525/27/28/34–37) fitted for a short time with a Thompson Diagram 117 boiler which had previously been fitted to one of the earlier A2/3s. These boilers were distinguishable by their round domes which were positioned farther forward than the 'banjo' domes.

G. W. Morrison

Plate 193: Bottom sees No. 60532 *Blue Peter* at Dundee in June 1965 with storm sheets over the cab. This was one of the five A2s which was fitted with a double chimney in 1949, none of which ever carried other than a Diagram 118 boiler. These five engines were also fitted with MLS multiple valve regulators and steam dryers. The operating rod for the four main valves and one pilot valve which were located transversely along the front of the superheater header can be seen on the side of the boiler above the handrail.

J. S. Whiteley

Plate 194: Above   A fine picture of No. 60530 *Sayajirao* passing Dunblane on 1st September 1965 with the 6.15pm Glasgow–Dundee. Only one A2, No. 60529, was initially allocated to Scotland, but between June and August 1949 Nos. 60525/27/28/31/37 were transferred to Aberdeen and Dundee to replace the Thompson A2/2s on the summer services. In November 1949 four more (Nos. 60532/34/35/36) were sent to Haymarket, with No. 60530 following in January 1950. From then on eleven A2s were allocated to the Scottish Region, three to the North Eastern Region (Nos. 60526/38/39) and one to the Eastern Region (No. 60533).

S. C. Crook

Plate 195: Top Right   In August 1964 No. 60535 *Hornets Beauty*, then allocated to Polmadie, is leaving Annan with the 11.00am Carlisle–Glasgow St. Enoch stopping train.

S. C. Crook

Plate 196: Bottom Right   From June 1961 until April 1966 No. 60528 *Tudor Minstrel* was allocated to Dundee, and is seen rather unusually in August 1965 on the Waverley route, nearing Riccarton Junction, with the 2.15pm Kingmoor–Millerhill freight.

S. C. Crook

Plate 197: Above No. 60529 *Pearl Diver* was allocated to Haymarket from new until October 1961 when it was moved to St. Margaret's, being withdrawn later the following year. Whilst at Haymarket it was used on Aberdeen expresses and is seen passing through Princes Street Gardens, Edinburgh on 25th June 1956 with a morning express from Aberdeen.

J. P. Wilson

Plate 198: Below The fireman seems to be hard at work on No. 60527 *Sun Chariot* as it leaves Perth with the up 'Grampian' on 22nd August 1963. The single chimney A2s were felt to be poor steamers, generally thought to be as a result of the self-cleaning apparatus in the smokebox which impaired the draughting, and over the years attempts were made to improve them, basically without much success. They had a tendency to be rather heavy on coal consumption and were considered to be inferior to the double chimney A2s. At several sheds they were not particularly popular with the crews, and in fact Ferryhill was given No. 60532 with double chimney in January 1951 to replace No. 60537 which had a single chimney, and which was a notoriously bad steamer.

S. C. Crook

Plate 199: Right On 13th July 1956 No. 60536 *Trimbush* of Haymarket is climbing Cowlairs Bank out of Glasgow Queen Street with the 11.00am to Edinburgh Waverley. The A2s were given the standard BR Brunswick green livery between May 1949 and August 1950.

G. W. Morrison

Plate 200: Below On 13th July 1960, No. 60534 *Irish Elegance* is awaiting departure from Carlisle with the 3.22pm to Edinburgh via the Waverley route.

T. Boustead

Plate 201: Above   Following the introduction of diesels, all the Haymarket A2s were moved to St. Margaret's late in 1961, and in September 1963 three were surprisingly transferred to Polmadie, Nos. 60527/30/35. No. 60535 *Hornets Beauty* is heading a Kilmarnock–Brent freight near Polquhap Summit on 28th May 1964 whilst still allocated to Polmadie.

D. Cross

Plate 202: Left   On 23rd April 1966 No. 60528 *Tudor Minstrel* is climbing to Shap Summit in pouring rain with a special railtour from Lancashire to Edinburgh via the Waverley route. By this date only three A2s were left, and No. 60528 was withdrawn only a few weeks later.

J. S. Whiteley

Plate 203: Above   Another special working is seen, on 28th March 1964, with No. 60527 *Sun Chariot* leaving Broughty Ferry with an Easter 'Scottish Rambler' railtour.

G. W. Morrison

Plate 204: Below   A sorry sight at Bathgate on 31st March 1964. No. 60529 *Pearl Diver* had been withdrawn in December 1962 and was awaiting cutting up.

G. W. Morrison

PEPPERCORN CLASS A1

BR No.	Name	Date Named	Built	Maker	Works No.	Withdrawn
60114	W. P. Allen	10/48	8/1948	Doncaster	2031	12/64
60115	Meg Merrilies	6/50	9/1948	Doncaster	2032	11/62
60116	Hal o' the Wynd	5/51	10/1948	Doncaster	2033	6/65
60117	Bois Roussel	7/50	10/1948	Doncaster	2034	6/65
60118	Archibald Sturrock	7/50	11/1948	Doncaster	2035	10/65
60119	Patrick Stirling	7/50	11/1948	Doncaster	2036	5/64
60120	Kittiwake	5/50	12/1948	Doncaster	2037	1/64
60121	Silurian	5/50	12/1948	Doncaster	2038	10/65
60122	Curlew	7/50	12/1948	Doncaster	2039	12/62
60123	H. A. Ivatt	7/50	2/1949	Doncaster	2040	10/62
60124	Kenilworth	8/50	3/1949	Doncaster	2041	3/66
60125	Scottish Union	1/51	4/1949	Doncaster	2043	7/64
60126	Sir Vincent Raven	8/50	4/1949	Doncaster	2042	1/65
60127	Wilson Worsdell	9/50	5/1949	Doncaster	2044	6/65
60128	Bongrace	11/50	5/1949	Doncaster	2045	1/65
60129	Guy Mannering	11/50	6/1949	Doncaster	2046	10/65
60130	Kestrel	7/50	9/1948	Darlington	2049	10/65
60131	Osprey	6/50	10/1948	Darlington	2050	10/65
60132	Marmion	12/50	10/1948	Darlington	2051	6/65
60133	Pommern	4/50	10/1948	Darlington	2052	6/65
60134	Foxhunter	10/50	11/1948	Darlington	2053	10/65
60135	Madge Wildfire	10/50	11/1948	Darlington	2054	11/62
60136	Alcazar	12/50	11/1948	Darlington	2055	5/63
60137	Redgauntlet	6/50	12/1948	Darlington	2056	10/62
60138	Boswell	9/50	12/1948	Darlington	2057	10/65
60139	Sea Eagle	5/50	12/1948	Darlington	2058	6/64
60140	Balmoral	7/50	12/1948	Darlington	2059	1/65
60141	Abbotsford	5/50	12/1948	Darlington	2060	10/64
60142	Edward Fletcher	10/50	2/1949	Darlington	2061	6/65
60143	Sir Walter Scott	9/50	2/1949	Darlington	2062	5/64
60144	King's Courier	1/51	3/1949	Darlington	2063	4/63
60145	Saint Mungo	8/50	3/1949	Darlington	2064	6/66
60146	Peregrine	12/50	4/1949	Darlington	2065	10/65
60147	North Eastern	3/52	4/1949	Darlington	2066	8/64
60148	Aboyeur	1/51	5/1949	Darlington	2067	6/65
60149	Amadis	12/50	5/1949	Darlington	2068	6/64
60150	Willbrook	1/51	6/1949	Darlington	2069	10/64
60151	Midlothian	3/51	6/1949	Darlington	2070	11/65
60152	Holyrood	6/51	7/1949	Darlington	2071	6/65
60153	Flamboyant	8/50	8/1949	Doncaster	2047	11/62
60154	Bon Accord	4/51	9/1949	Doncaster	2048	10/65
60155	Borderer	3/51	9/1949	Doncaster	2049	10/65
60156	Great Central	7/52	10/1949	Doncaster	2050	5/65
60157	Great Eastern	11/51	11/1949	Doncaster	2051	1/65
60158	Aberdonian	3/51	11/1949	Doncaster	2052	12/64
60159	Bonnie Dundee	7/51	11/1949	Doncaster	2053	10/63
60160	Auld Reekie	3/51	12/1949	Doncaster	2054	12/63
60161	North British	6/51	12/1949	Doncaster	2055	10/63
60162	Saint Johnstoun	8/51	12/1949	Doncaster	2056	10/63

When Edward Thompson retired in June 1946 sixteen standard Class A1 Pacifics were on order from Doncaster Works and twenty-three had been authorised for construction at Darlington. Prior to his retirement various drawings had been prepared for the production A1s, some based on his rebuilt *Great Northern* and some as partially streamlined engines. However, after Peppercorn had taken up office further drawings for the A1 Pacifics were prepared and these dispensed with the previous proposals for streamlining. He did, however, retain many of Thompson's ideas in his 6 feet 8 inches Pacific such as divided drive, separate valve gears for each of the three 19" x 26" cylinders and the large redesigned Thompson style Diagram 118 boiler which had been fitted to Peppercorn's earlier A2s. It was not until as late as May 1948, only a few months before the first A1s were completed, that a decision was taken to replace the intended single chimney with a Kylchap double blastpipe and chimney.

In August 1948 the first A1, No. 60114, entered traffic, and it was then that the final batch of ten A1s were ordered from Doncaster. These were completed during 1949, shortly before Peppercorn retired as CME Eastern and North Eastern Region of British Railways on 31st December 1949.

All forty-nine A1s were built in sixteen months and were immediately put to work on the East Coast main line, performing consistently well on some of the heaviest trains. They were strong, sure-footed engines, but they did gain a reputation for rough riding characteristics compared to the smooth running Gresley Pacifics. Dieselisation resulted in the Peppercorn A1s having an average life of only about fifteen years, and sadly none has been preserved.

Plate 205: Above A proud moment at Darlington in September 1948 on completion of their first A1 Pacific No. 60130, later named *Kestrel*. All the A1s except the last thirteen from Doncaster, Nos. 60127–9 and 60153–62, were turned out in full LNER green livery with black and white lining, but none ever carried the lettering LNER on the tender as they appeared after nationalisation.

Courtesy National Railway Museum

Plate 206: Below No. 60125, later named *Scottish Union*, is approaching Grantham with a down freight on 7th May 1949. This engine had recently been completed at Doncaster and was running in, having just been allocated to Doncaster. All the Doncaster built A1s had tenders and cabs with snap-head rivets, and those from Darlington had countersunk rivets. Most of the A1s had electric lighting equipment fitted when they were built, with a Stone's turbo generator which can be seen inside the right-hand smoke deflector.

J. P. Wilson

Plate 207: Above   The last thirteen A1s built at Doncaster were given a new blue livery with black and white lining. The cab sides included the lining, and the tender incorporated the BR lion and wheel emblem. No. 60148 *Aboyeur* was given this blue livery in January 1951 when it was named, and is seen at Grantham on 28th March 1951.

J. P. Wilson

Plate 208: Below   All the thirty-six A1s which were initially given LNER green livery had been given BR blue by June 1951 as they passed through Works. No. 60121 *Silurian* is in blue livery as it passes Greenwood on 5th June 1950 heading the up 'Scarborough Flyer'. Only the first A1, No. 60114, was named shortly after entering traffic, and the remainder were named between April 1950 and July 1952.

A. C. Cawston

Plate 209: *Right* The A1s did not retain their blue livery for very long, and from August 1951 they were given the standard Brunswick green with orange and black lining, the last one being No. 60160 in March 1953. No. 60134 *Foxhunter* is seen near Brookmans Park on 27th September 1953 heading an up Leeds excursion. The tender still carries the early BR emblem but the original Thompson beaded chimney has been replaced by a lipped chimney. The original positioning of the smokebox numberplate can be seen above the handrail and the top hinge. From October 1954 this was repositioned on the hinge itself, enabling the top lamp iron to be lowered.

N. Sprinks

BR GREEN

Plate 211: *Below* In July 1958, *Great Eastern* is seen again, at Potters Bar, with a Leeds express. This was one of four A1s to be named after LNER constituent companies, and the nameplates of these four engines incorporated the appropriate hand-painted coat of arms.

D. Cross

Plate 210: *Above* No. 60157 *Great Eastern* is near Brookmans Park in July 1959 with a Kings Cross—Leeds express. The later BR emblem can be seen on the tender. This was one of five A1s (Nos. 60153—57) which were equipped with Timken roller bearings on all their axles which succeeded in increasing their mileages between heavy repairs. These five engines retained these axle boxes to the end, but no other engines had them fitted.

D. Cross

Plate 212: Above   In September 1958 No. 60130 *Kestrel* of Copley Hill is leaving Kings Cross with the down 'West Riding'.
C. R. L. Coles

Plate 213: Below   No. 60133 *Pommern* heads north near Oakleigh Park on 13th September 1960 with a Leeds express.
D. Cross

PEPPERCORN A1s IN SERVICE

Plate 214: Right Copley Hill initially received five A1s for through workings to London, but by late 1951 this allocation had been increased to ten. On 22nd March 1949 No. 60131, later named *Osprey*, is leaving Grantham with a down Leeds express.

J. P. Wilson

Plate 215: Below No. 60123 *H. A. Ivatt* is passing Greenwood on 22nd June 1953 with the down 'West Riding', formed of several coaches from one of the pre-war streamlined expresses which can be seen at the front of the train. At this period No. 60123 was allocated to Ardsley and would not generally be used on this working, as a rule returning to Leeds on the 1.18pm express from Kings Cross, having probably worked up on a parcels train.

A. C. Cawston

Two pages of pictures of A1s on shed at York. *Plate 216: Above* shows No. 60141 *Abbotsford* in the shed yard on 30th August 1964. This engine was shedded at York when first delivered, spent about 6 months at Kings Cross 1949/50, and about thirteen years at Copley Hill from May 1950 until September 1963, when it returned to York until withdrawal.

G. W. Morrison

Plate 217: Below   Nos. 60150 *Willbrook* and 60121 *Silurian* are inside the roundhouse on 2nd May 1964. This building now forms part of the National Railway Museum housing the National Collection.

J. S. Whiteley

Plate 218: Right
Another view of No. 60150 *Willbrook* inside the roundhouse. The York A1s were mainly used on Newcastle trains, and their diagrams only rarely took them to Kings Cross, except in the case of engine failures.

J. S. Whiteley

Plate 219: Below
Another view inside the roundhouse at York sees No. 60120 *Kittiwake* on 19th October 1963. This engine was built at Doncaster and the snap-head rivets on the cab and tender can clearly be seen. The route availability RA 9, can be seen painted on the cab side.

J. S. Whiteley

Plate 220: *Above* No. 60124 *Kenilworth* is leaving Peterborough in 1964 with a down express.

S. C. Crook

Plate 221: *Left* Ardsley A1 No. 60123 *H. A. Ivatt* is passing Lincoln Central on 1st June 1957 with a down Leeds express, diverted from the East Coast main line because of engineering work.

J. P. Wilson

Plate 222: Above   A busy scene at Grantham on 4th October 1952, the centre piece being No. 60120 *Kittiwake* of Copley Hill leaving with a down Leeds express.

J. P. Wilson

Plate 223: Below   No. 60145 *Saint Mungo* is restarting from its Peterborough stop with a down express in 1964.

S. C. Crook

Plate 224: Left A Leeds–Kings Cross express is climbing towards Stoke Tunnel on 7th July 1962 behind No. 60134 *Foxhunter* of Copley Hill.

G. W. Morrison

Plate 225: Below Another Leeds–Kings Cross express is seen this time just south of Grantham and starting its climb to Stoke Tunnel, behind No. 60118 *Archibald Sturrock*, also one of Copley Hill's A1s.

T. Boustead

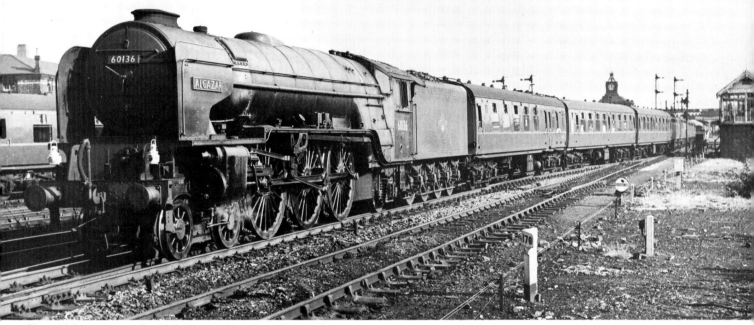

Plate 226: *Above* On 24th August 1961 No. 60136 *Alcazar* is leaving Wakefield Westgate with a Kings Cross-Leeds express. This was one of sixteen A1s which at one time from 1955 was fitted with a Diagram 117 boiler, and No. 60136 was fitted with one from March 1961 until withdrawal in May 1963. The round domes on the Diagram 117 boilers were farther forward, and when fitted to the A1s these domes were usually hidden under a dummy 'banjo' dome.

G. W. Morrison

Plate 227: *Below* No. 60149 *Amadis* is shunting the Hull portion of an up express at Doncaster on 24th March 1963. Together with several other A1s, No. 60149 returned to Doncaster in the late 1950s after being replaced by diesels on express duties elsewhere, and for several years an A1 could be seen on standby duties just to the south of Doncaster station.

G. W. Morrison

During the entire existence of the A1s, they were a familiar sight in Leeds at the head of Kings Cross expresses, predominating over other classes of LNER Pacifics.

Plate 228: *Above* shows No. 60148 *Aboyeur* of Copley Hill climbing away from Leeds Central with the 9.42am to Kings Cross on 14th May 1963, with the curvature of the track disguising the length of the train.

J. S. Whiteley

Plate 229: *Below*   On 6th June 1962 Doncaster A1 No. 60125 *Scottish Union* is getting into its stride at Beeston Junction with the 10.10am from Leeds Central.

G. W. Morrison

Plate 230: Above No. 60136 *Alcazar* is returning to its home base at Doncaster with the 2.05pm local from Leeds Central. It is approaching Holbeck High Level, shortly after leaving Leeds Central on 30th June 1961, with Farnley Junction 'Jinty' No. 47570 shunting alongside.

G. W. Morrison

Plate 231: Right Some of the paintwork on No. 60117 *Bois Roussel* is looking decidedly the worse for wear on 25th April 1964 as it awaits departure from Leeds Central with the 5.10pm to Doncaster.

J. S. Whiteley

Plate 232: Below Another picture of *Bois Roussel* of Copley Hill, this time shortly after passing Holbeck High Level with the Sunday 4.40pm to Kings Cross on 1st July 1962. The lines to the left are to Bradford, and in the centre, the approach to Copley Hill MPD.

J. S. Whiteley

Plate 233: Above   Another Copley Hill stalwart, No. 60134 *Foxhunter*, standing at Leeds Central with the 12.30pm to Kings Cross on 16th March 1962.

G. W. Morrison

Plate 234: Below   A somewhat deserted Copley Hill MPD can be seen in the background of this picture of No. 60145 *Saint Mungo* heading the 9.42am to Kings Cross on 19th March 1963.

J. S. Whiteley

Three pictures of A1s on shed. *Plate 235: Above* shows No. 60150 *Willbrook* on the ashpits at York on 6th February 1964. *G. W. Morrison.* No. 60145 *Saint Mungo* is seen in *Plate 236: Right* standing outside Copley Hill on 19th August 1961. *G. W. Morrison* and *Plate 237: Below* shows No. 60147 *North Eastern* over the ashpits at York on 11th June 1964. This picture shows the NER coat of arms incorporated in the nameplate. *G. W. Morrison*

Plate 238: Above   On 29th April 1962 No. 60122 *Curlew* rests between duties at Doncaster. This picture clearly shows the later emblem on the tender which BR adopted from the late 1950s.

G. W. Morrison

Plate 239: Below   Another picture at Doncaster, this time of No. 60121 *Silurian* awaiting painting after an overhaul at Doncaster Works, on 5th May 1962. The electric lighting equipment has been removed and it is temporarily attached to a six-wheeled V2 tender. No. 60121 was one of twenty-one A1s which, between December 1961 and May 1963, were fitted with a divided handrail on the smokebox door with the lamp iron positioned between them.

G. W. Morrison

Plate 240: Above By August 1964 No. 60152 *Holyrood* had been moved to St. Margaret's from Haymarket where it had been for ten years. After being moved it was relegated to secondary duties and is seen leaving Carlisle with the 2.15pm freight to Millerhill.

S. C. Crook

Plate 241: Right The Kings Cross Yards—Niddrie 'Scotch Goods' is seen crossing the River Trent, north of Newark, on 23rd August 1958 behind No. 60158 *Aberdonian*, one of the roller bearing engines.

T. Boustead

Plate 242: Left　No. 60152 *Holyrood* spent most of its life at Haymarket and was used in common with their other A1s on main line duties, seldom venturing farther south than Newcastle. On 17th July 1961 it is emerging from Mound Tunnel, shortly after leaving Waverley station with the 5.25pm to Dundee.

J. S. Whiteley

Plate 243: Above　On Whit Saturday 5th June 1965 No. 60154 *Bon Accord* is a long way from its home depot of Neville Hill as it passes Dalry Junction with a Bradford—Glasgow relief, having travelled via Carlisle and Kilmarnock.

D. Cross

Plate 244: Left　An evening scene inside Edinburgh Waverley on 22nd July 1963 with No. 60142 *Edward Fletcher* of Tweedmouth awaiting departure on the 10.10pm sleeper to Kings Cross. Ten A1s were sent to Tweedmouth in September 1962 where they were mainly confined to freight work before most of them were transferred to Gateshead.

J. S. Whiteley

Plate 245: Above   The Heaton A1s were seldom seen on the Waverley route, but in April 1962 one of them, in the form of 60132 *Marmion*, is leaving Riddings, junction of the Langholm branch which can be seen on the right-hand side of the picture. It is heading the 9.20 am Carlisle–Edinburgh Waverley.

S. C. Crook

Plate 246: Below   The St. Margaret's A1s were often used over the Waverley route on both passenger and freight, and No. 60152 *Holyrood* is seen near Falahill Summit on 5th September 1963, just after being moved from Haymarket to St. Margaret's, heading a Millerhill–Kingmoor freight.

D. Cross

Plate 247: Above　On 27th July 1964 No. 60131 *Osprey* of Neville Hill nears Brackenhill Junction, near Mauchline on the former G&SWR, with the 2.00pm Glasgow St. Enoch–Carlisle stopping train. Five A1s (Nos. 60118/31/34/46/54) were transferred to Neville Hill in July 1963 and occasionally were used on turns to Glasgow, usually returning south on this working.

D. Cross

Plate 248: Below　In September 1963 No. 60152 *Holyrood* passes Lady Victoria Pit, Gorebridge, on the Waverley route with a Millerhill–Kingmoor freight.

D. Cross

Plate 249: Above The prestige Pullman workings were often entrusted to the A1s, and in this picture No. 60123 *H. A. Ivatt* climbs sedately out of Leeds at Wortley South Junction with the up 'Queen of Scots' on 9th July 1960.

G. W. Morrison

Plate 250: Below Copley Hill A1 No. 60139 *Sea Eagle* emerges from Peascliffe Tunnel with the up 'Yorkshire Pullman' in 1955. At this period a Copley Hill crew worked to Kings Cross on this train and returned to Leeds the same day with the 3.45pm 'West Riding', a daily turn of 372 miles.

M. W. Earley

Plate 251: Left In Autumn 1961 the line between Leeds and Wakefield was closed due to engineering works on several Sundays, and through carriages from Bradford to Kings Cross were diverted via Low Moor with Pacific haulage from Bradford. No. 60118 *Archibald Sturrock* is climbing away from Bradford Exchange station on Sunday, 8th October 1961 with an afternoon train to Kings Cross.

G. W. Morrison

Plate 252: Below A1s were only rarely seen on the Settle and Carlisle line, towards the end of their careers. No. 60118 *Archibald Sturrock* is seen again, this time approaching Ais Gill Summit on 4th July 1964 with an up CTAC special from Gourock.

G. W. Morrison

137

Plate 253: Right On 28th September 1963 No. 60114 *W. P. Allen* is seen in unfamiliar surroundings, at Sowerby Bridge, as it prepares to leave with an excursion to Blackpool Illuminations. This was the first Peppercorn A1 to be completed, and it had the distinction of being named shortly after entering service, the remainder of the A1s having to wait some time before being given names. It was named after a driver who had progressed from a cleaner on the GNR and who became a trade union member of the Railway Executive. This engine also differed from the other A1s in having the bogie which had been intended for A2 No. 60539, which was to a slightly different design.

G. W. Morrison

Plate 254: Below Towards the end of their careers several A1s were used on specially organised railtours. No. 60131 *Osprey* is about to leave Leeds City on Sunday 21st March 1965 with the RCTS Tyne–Solway Tour.

G. W. Morrison

Plate 255: Left No. 60131 i leaving Leeds at Whitehall Junctioi on 31st July 1965 with a relie Newcastle train, the nameplate having been removed in antici pation of imminent withdrawal By this time the A1s had beer replaced by diesels on front line work and were to be found on variety of mundane workings.

J. S. Whiteley

Plate 256: Below Ardsley A1 No. 60123 *H. A. Ivatt* suffered premature withdrawal in October 1962 after being severely damaged in a collision near Offord, just south of Huntingdon on 7th September whilst working the 8.50pm Kings Cross—Leeds freight. The extent of the damage can be seen in this picture taken outside Doncaster Works on 29th September 1962. Withdrawal of the A1s began in earnest late in 1962, and by the end of the year six had been withdrawn, including No. 60123. During 1963 six more were withdrawn, and eleven more during 1964. By January 1965 the twenty-six survivors were at Doncaster, Gateshead, Ardsley, Neville Hill and York. The two Doncaster engines were both withdrawn during January, and by the end of the year there were only two survivors, Nos. 60124 and 60145, both at Darlington for use on standby duties. They were both withdrawn in March 1966, but No. 60145 was reinstated on 17th April 1966 and sent to York, where it was finally withdrawn in June 1966 bringing to an end the short reign of the Peppercorn A1s, thought by many to be the most reliable of the Pacifics designed at Doncaster, although rarely partici- pating in the glamorous exploits of the Gresley Pacifics.

G. W. Morrison

GRESLEY CLASS A1

Boiler pressure		180 lb/sq in.
Grate area		41.25 sq ft.
Weight:	Engine	92 tons 9 cwt.
	GNR tender	56 tons 6 cwt.
	Corridor tender	62 tons 8 cwt.
	New type non-corridor	57 tons 18 cwt.
	Streamlined non-corridor	60 tons 7 cwt. (from May 1938)
Engine wheelbase		35' 9"
Tender wheelbase		16' 0" (all types)
Total length over buffers		70' 5⅛ " (with GNR tender)
		70' 2⅜ " (corridor)
		70' 5⅛ " (New type non-corridor)
		70' 5⅛ " (Streamlined non-corridor)
Driving Wheels		6' 8"
Cylinders		Three 20" x 26"
Motion		Walschaerts/Gresley with 8" piston valves

RAVEN CLASS A2

			No. 2404 as rebuilt
Boiler pressure		200 lb/sq in.	180 lb/sq in.
Grate area		41.5 sq ft.	41.25 sq ft.
Weight:	Engine	101 tons 10 cwt.	98 tons
	Six-wheeled tender	46 tons 12 cwt.	57 tons 18 cwt (8-wheeled)
Engine wheelbase		37' 2"	37' 2"
Tender wheelbase		12' 8" (6-wheeled)	16' 1½" (8-wheeled)
Total length over buffers		72' 7¼"	74' 8⅛ (with 8-wheeled tender)
Driving wheels		6' 8"	6' 8"
Cylinders		Three 19" x 26"	Three 19" x 26"
Motion		Stephenson with 8¾" piston valves	Stephenson with 8¾" piston valves

THOMPSON CLASS A2/3

Boiler pressure		250 lb/sq in.
Grate area		50 sq ft.
Weight:	Engine	101 tons 10 cwt.
	Tender	60 tons 7 cwt.
Engine wheelbase		36' 11"
Tender wheelbase		16' 0"
Total length over buffers		72' 10¾"
Driving wheels		6' 2"
Cylinders		Three 19" x 26"
Motion		Walschaerts with 10" piston valves

THOMPSO

Boiler pressure
Grate area
Weight: Engine
          Tender
Engine wheelbase
Tender wheelbase
Total length over b
Driving wheels
Cylinders
Motion

THOMPSO

Boiler pressure
Grate area
Weight: Engine
          Six-whee
          Eight-wh
Engine wheelbase
Six-wheeled tender
Eight-wheeled tend
Total length over b

Driving wheels
Cylinders
Motion

PEPPERCO

Boiler pressure
Grate area
Weight: Engine

          Tender

Engine wheelbase
Tender wheelbase
Total length over b
Driving wheels
Cylinders
Motion